Reconsidering Braddock's Road to Martin's

By Lannie Dietle

Copyright © 2017 by Lannie Dietle

Published by: **Cumberland Heritage Foundation**
28 Washington Street,
Cumberland, Maryland 21502

Cover image: "**A map of the country between Will's Creek & Monongahela River shewing the rout and encampments of the English army in 1755**"

This book is dedicated to Robert L. Bantz, in honor of his long-term commitment to identifying and preserving surviving portions of Braddock's road, and his long-term commitment to history education.

History is written for the most part from the outside. Truth often suffers distortion by reason of the point of view of the narrator, some pre-occupation of his judgment or fancy not only as to relative merits but even as to facts in their real relations.

Major-General Joshua Lawrence Chamberlain, in "**The Passing of the Armies**", 1915.

Table of Contents

1. Introduction — 1
2. Conventional wisdom — 5
3. Post-1755 improvements to Braddock's road — 17
4. Alterations that became known as Braddock's road — 23
5. Nemacolin's Ohio Company road — 31
6. Gist was involved with opening the Ohio Company road — 41
7. Washington followed the Ohio Company road in 1753 — 45
8. Washington improved the Ohio Company road in 1754 — 49
9. Participant expedition maps — 53
10. Subsequent mid-1700s maps — 69
11. Martin's plantation — 81
12. More recent documents — 87
13. A perplexing 1756 letter from Thomas Cresap — 97
14. The fly in the ointment: The 1760 Mountain survey — 99
15. Local tradition — 101
16. Conclusion — 105
17. Epilogue — 107

Author's Preface

Origin of the research

This book began as an internet-based group discussion of a 1760 survey that mentions Braddock's road in a most-perplexing way. Over time, members of the group presented a wide variety of information concerning the route of Braddock's expedition. As I reviewed this information, I realized that the conventional wisdom concerning the route of the expedition near Frostburg, Maryland and the location Braddock's second camp were contrary to core documentary evidence. When I pointed this out, several group members were surprised they hadn't noticed the discrepancies themselves. I began to explore the discrepancies in more depth by developing a monograph on the subject that was shared with the group. The interest in the theory that document presented encouraged me to reorganize the material and create this modest book, so the theory can be more widely shared, and scrutinized.

About the author

My wife Cheryl and I live in Houston, Texas, and plan to retire in Annapolis, Maryland next year. I am employed at an engineering firm in Texas, where I have worked with the design and implementation of rotary seals since 1982. My ancestral roots are in the various southern townships of Somerset County, Pennsylvania. My earliest memories were formed near the Mason-Dixon line, and the region still feels like home. My interest in history began as a youth, from discussions with my grandparents, and the chance purchase of two mid-1860s books at a rural auction. My interest in primitive roads can be traced back to a youthful encounter with an abandoned road near the top of Savage Mountain, and a broken wagon axle that was found submerged at an old fording site.

Previous research

Several decades of Somerset County genealogical studies provided useful knowledge of the area, despite not having lived there since the late 1950s. These studies resulted in a book on my paternal family line, and an extensive website on my maternal line. To develop material for the website, I worked closely with Michael McKenzie of Barrelville to jointly research a number of Southampton Township historical topics. Following our extensive Southampton Township work, Mr. McKenzie identified a new objective: To research and promote the history of nearby areas of Allegany County, Maryland that he felt were underrepresented in published literature. This steered our collaborative research effort in a direction that ultimately led to writing the book "**In Search of the Turkey Foot Road**". The intensive effort required to understand the history and route of the Turkey Foot Road, which began at Fort Cumberland, provided the preliminary background in early regional history that was critical to writing "**Fort Cumberland: The missing years**". The knowledge gained from writing those two books provided a basis for interpreting the information I encountered concerning Braddock's road.

Acknowledgements

This historical study, like any field of study, rides on the shoulders of individuals from earlier generations who took the time to document their labors and observations. I owe the authors, diarists, and cartographers whose work I draw from a tremendous debt of gratitude.

I thank the Cumberland Heritage Foundation for their interest in publishing this material. I also thank the individuals recognized in the footnotes who have provided assistance in one way or another. I gratefully acknowledge the help received, and do not mean to imply that they endorse my research and conclusions.

1. Introduction

A brief introduction to the historical period

The Ohio Company was granted the right to a vast quantity of land along the Ohio if they could settle it.[1] They built a storehouse along the Potomac River, at the mouth of Wills Creek (now Ridgeley, West Virginia) as a base of operations. The Ohio Company financed road construction west from Wills Creek, passing through the Allegheny Mountains, in order to facilitate trade with the Indians, and to promote western settlement.

English trading activities in the region drained by the Ohio River caused the French to take various steps to enforce their claim to the region. Some of these steps included attacking the English trading post at the Twightwee[2] town of Pickawillany[3] in 1752, and building Fort Presque Isle, Fort Le Boeuf, and Fort Machault.

The English decided to build a fort at the present-day location of Pittsburgh to oppose the French, after being requested to do so by Indians from that region. Colonel Trent's forces arrived there in early 1754 for construction activities. A French military force expelled Trent's forces in April of 1754, and built Fort Duquesne. This fort blocked British trading routes, and dominated the confluence of the Allegheny and Monongahela rivers. The French attacked Logstown in May of 1754.[4] Ensuing events led to Captain Jumonville's fatal encounter with George Washington, the battle of Fort Necessity, and the construction of Fort Cumberland. Braddock used Fort Cumberland as his base of operations during his flawed and ultimately disastrous campaign against the French at Fort Duquesne. The leading elements of Braddock's army set off from Fort Cumberland to advance against Fort Duquesne on May 29, 1755, generally following the Ohio Company road. England did not declare war on France until May 17, 1756, long after Braddock's defeat.

Fort Duquesne was ultimately captured in November, 1758 by the Forbes expedition.

---

[1] See the second petition of the Ohio Company.

[2] Although this nation of Indians is typically referred to as *"Twightwee"* in early British writings, their autonym is *"Miami"*.

[3] Reportedly, the Twightwee Indian town of Pickawillany was about 29 miles north of present-day Dayton Ohio. An archaeological dig was taking place at the site of Pickawillany in 2011, according to reporter Tom Millhouse.

[4] The Logstown attack is described in a May 24, 1754 letter that was written from Philadelphia. Although not documentary evidence, Volume 2 of the 1826 book **"The Universal Chronologist"** gives the date of the Logstown attack as May 14, 1754, stating, "*M. De Contrecoeur destroyed Loggs Town, in North America.*" In his book, "**Indian Paths of Pennsylvania**", Wallace describes Logstown as being at Legionville, Pennsylvania, which is about 7 miles south of Rochester and the mouth of Beaver River. This agrees with the 1755 Mitchell map, which describes Logstown as *"built & Settled by the English several Years agoe."* On present-day roads, which follow the river, it is 18.4 miles from Legionville to the Route 279 bridge at the point in Pittsburgh.

This book presents a theory regarding the route between Clarysville and the second camp

The route of General Braddock's march westward from Fort Cumberland in 1755 has intrigued historians for generations. The first camp of the expedition was referred to as Grove Camp,[5] and the second camp was at a place called Martin's plantation that was located within the Georges Creek watershed.

Over the last 105 years, a consensus has formed regarding the route taken between the two camps, and the location of the second camp. This consensus is based on research performed by John Kennedy Lacock early in the twentieth century. The consensus route follows Braddock Run to Clarysville, and then follows Hoffman Hollow — the valley3 of a tributary of Preston Run that Route 68 (the National Freeway) now follows.

This book was written to present information suggesting that Braddock's line of march may have turned northwest at Clarysville, following the valley of Porter Run toward the village of Eckhart Mines that alternate Route 40 now follows, and then continued on to the second camp. This postulated route is presented as nothing more than a theory[6] to be studied and dissected, hopefully leading to someone finding hard evidence that either affirms or refutes the theory. I will be delighted if someone reading this book is inspired to find such evidence, whatever the outcome. Such evidence is most likely to be found in old deeds and surveys. In the meantime, it may be imprudent to enthusiastically accept the theory presented herein, since it is based primarily on map analysis.

Preston Run and Porter Run are the head forks of Braddock Run. These two streams join together to form Braddock Run at Clarysville. The terrain in the general area of interest is shown by an 1898 topographical map that is included as Figure 1.

---

[5] Orme's account of Braddock's expedition refers to the first camp as *"Spendelow Camp"*. Although not documentary evidence, the Maryland Historical Trust Inventory Form for State Historic Sites Survey No. AL-V-B-099 indicates that Spendelow Camp was located approximately at latitude 39.633970°, longitude -78.833194°, along Braddock Run.

[6] I don't like writing about theories, because I know all too well that I not infallible. I dedicated a chapter of the book **"In Search of the Turkey Foot Road"** to a wonderful theory that was reviewed by one of the world's foremost living experts on the antique map the theory was based on: The 1755 Fry and Jefferson map. I later proved that wonderful theory to be dead wrong using documentary evidence. After that dreadful experience, and other similar experiences, this book is way outside of my comfort zone, but the theory it presents seems worth sharing to stimulate further research. As you read this, be fully aware that I have the proven ability to write theories very convincingly, even when I'm wrong.

Reconsidering Braddock's Road to Martin's

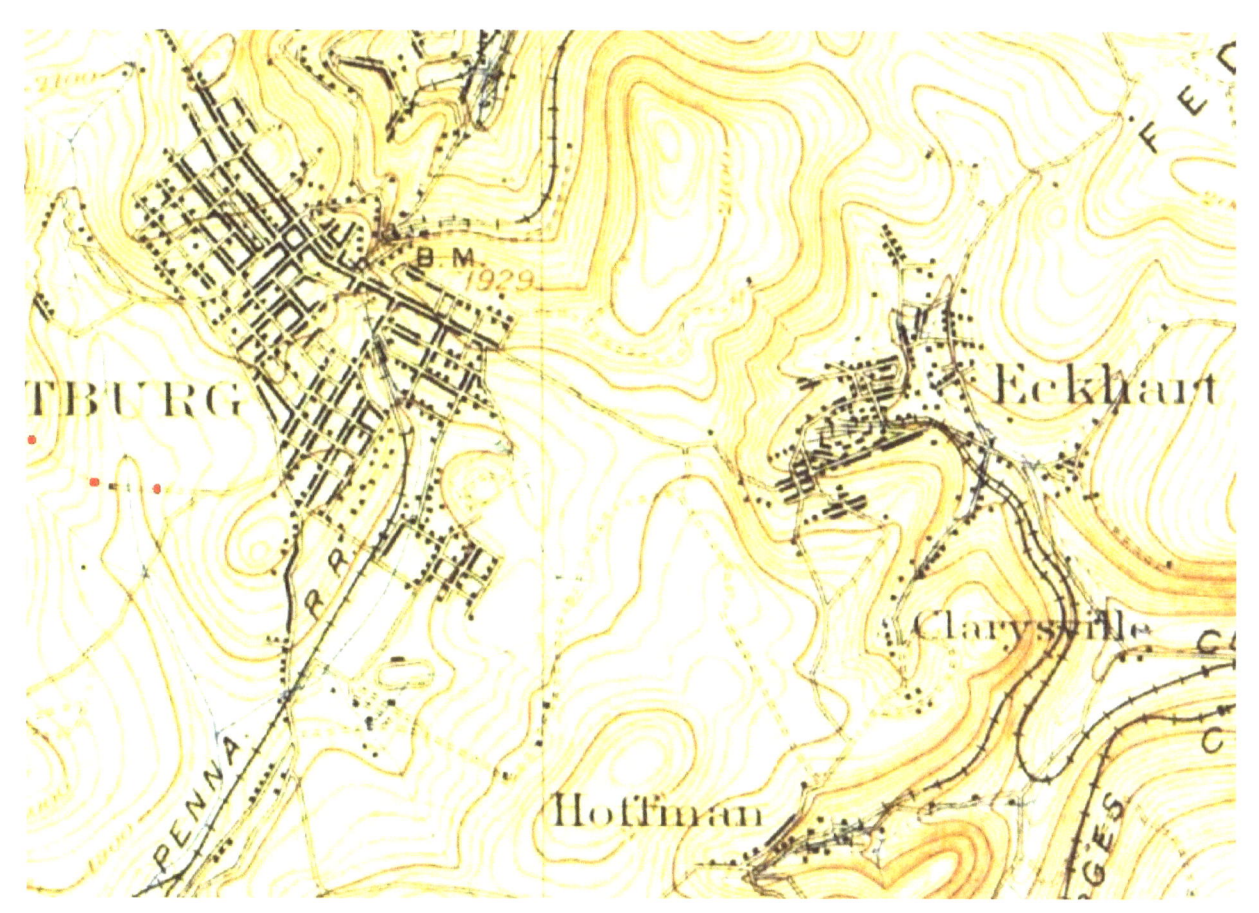

Figure 1 — This is a portion of an 1898 topographical map that covers the area this book focuses on. The traditional route of Braddock's road westward from Frostburg is highlighted with red dots. The black rectangle between two of the red dots may represent Musselman's 1806 springhouse. Porter Run flows southeast from the village of Eckhart Mines, joining Preston Run at Clarysville to form Braddock Run, a tributary of Wills Creek, which in turn flows into the North Branch of the Potomac River at Cumberland. Preston Run begins at Vale Summit. A tributary of Preston Run flows through Hoffman Hollow, and joins Preston Run one-half-mile from the mouth of Preston Run. In 1898, most of Frostburg was located between the head forks of Georges Creek, a tributary of the North Branch of the Potomac River. The mouth of Georges Creek is at Westernport. The premise of this book is that Braddock's expedition followed the valley of Porter Run, instead of following Preston Run and Hoffman Hollow.

2. Conventional wisdom

Atkinson's study of Braddock's road

The first intensive study of Braddock's route was conducted by Civil Engineer T.C. Atkinson of Cumberland, Maryland in the mid-1800s, which resulted in a well-known route map that was created by Mr. Middleton.[7] The relevant section of this map is included as Figure 2, and has been rotated so that north is at the top. On Middleton's map, Atkinson's projected route of Braddock's expedition is shown as a dotted line, and the now-old National Road is shown as a bold double line.

Middleton did not include Spendelow's alternate route to the first camp via the Narrows, but this omission is immaterial to the present subject. Middleton's map shows the line of march as following Braddock Run, and then passing south of a hill that is located just west of Clarysville. As Middleton's map illustrates, the old National Road passes north of this hill on the way to the village of Eckhart Mines, and Frostburg. After the hill, Middleton shows Braddock's route passing well-south of the location of the then-small village of Frostburg, and crossing over Savage Mountain well-south of the National Road. The locations of Braddock's camps are not shown.

Atkinson describes[8] the road crossing what was then known as Wills Mountain[9] (just west of Cumberland), and then states:

> ...*I have thought it time not idly spent to attempt to pursue its scattered traces as far as it is in my power, among more pressing occupations. In this sketch I do not design to pursue it to its extent, but only to identify it in those parts where it has been convenient for me to visit it, and in others to shadow out its general direction. Where it is obscure I hope to have opportunities to examine it at a future day. ...*
>
> *For reasons not easy to divine, the route across Will's Mountain, first adopted for the National Road was selected, instead of the more favorable one through the narrows of Will's Creek, to which the road has been changed within a few years, for the purpose of avoiding that formidable ascent. The traces are very distinct on the East and West slopes, the modern road crossing it frequently. From the Western foot, the route continued up Braddock's Run to the forks of the stream, where Clary's Tavern now stands, 9 miles from Cumberland, when it turned to the left, in order to reach a point on the ridge favorable to an easy descent into the valley of George's Creek. It is surprising that having reached this high ground, the favorable spur by which the National Road accomplishes the ascent of the Great Savage Mountain, did not strike the attention of the engineers, as the labor requisite to surmount the barrier from the deep valley of George's Creek, must have contributed greatly to those bitter complaints which Braddock made*

---

[7] Mr. Middleton was one of Mr. Atkinson's assistants during a survey for the Pittsburgh and Connellsville Railroad.

[8] Atkinson's treatise was published in an 1847 issue of "**The Olden Times**", and was reprinted in Lowdermilk's 1878 book "**The History of Cumberland...**" This means that his research was conducted before the unfaithful version of the *"Orme map"* of Braddock's expedition (bottom of Figure 20) was published in Winthrop Sargent's 1855 book "**The History of an Expedition against fort Du Quesne, in 1755...**"

[9] This portion of Wills Mountain is now known as Haystack Mountain.

against the Colonial Governments for their failure to assist him more effectively in the transportation department.

Passing then a mile to the South of Frostburg, the road approaches the East foot of Savage Mountain, which it crosses about one mile South of the National Road, and thence by very favorable ground through the dense forests of white pine peculiar to this region, it got to the North of the National Road, near the gloomy tract called the "Shades of Death." This was the 15th of June, when the dense gloom of the summer woods, and the favorable shelter which these enormous pines would give an Indian enemy, must have made a most sensible impression on all minds, of the insecurity of their mode of advance.

Atkinson does not describe what evidence he found that led him to conclude that Braddock took the left-hand valley at Clary's Tavern (now Clarysville). Atkinson's overall route seems questionable, in view of the traditional route of Braddock's road through Frostburg, which is still visible just east of Spring Street and is referenced in a 1793 law, as described later in this book.

Lacock's study of Braddock's road

The second intensive study of Braddock's route was conducted by John Kennedy Lacock,[10] and was published in book form as "**Braddock Road**" in 1912. The book includes a map of Lacock's projected route, and the relevant portion of that map is included herein as Figure 3.

In regard to the portion of the route that is the topic of this book, Lacock wrote:

At Clarysville the road turns into the valley of Flaggy Run,[11] apparently following the west bank of the stream,[12] along which there is a deep depression formed by an old mill race that might easily be mistaken for the road itself. About half a mile southwest of Clarysville the road turns almost at a right angle, keeping approximately the course of the present county road for three-quarters of a mile up Hoffman Hollow.[13] Here again, running parallel to the present road, is an old tramway roadbed which might readily be taken for Braddock's path. A short distance beyond the Hoffman coal mines, on the north side of the road, is a very deep scar, which is probably a part of Braddock's roadbed. At the top of the hill the road turns northward at almost a right angle in order to avoid what was formerly a very wide swamp, and then passes over the ridge and down through Layman's orchard, where there is a deep scar.[14] Near the end of this ridge, overlooking Frostburg and about five miles from Spendelow Camp, is the site of the second encampment, Martin's Plantation.[15]

---

[10] For an extensive biography of John Kennedy Lacock, see Volume 3 of the 1914 book "**Encyclopedia of Pennsylvania Biography**".

[11] This passage makes it clear that Flaggy Run was an older name for the stream that is now known as Preston Run.

[12] Lacock's footnote here states, *"See Middleton's map."*

[13] One may reasonably suspect that Lacock is describing an antecedent to the county road that appears on the 1898 map shown in Figure 1. The 1760 Mountain survey, quoted later in this book, suggests that such an antecedent route may have already existed in 1760.

[14] Postcard No. 11 in Lacock's Braddock Road postcard series shows this scar, proving the existence of an abandoned road.

[15] Lacock's footnote here is, "*Orme Journal*, 333."

From here the road crosses first the headwaters of the eastern branch of George's Creek, next the Cumberland and Pennsylvania Railroad, and then runs southeast of Frostburg into the premises of James Grose, and on through the Sheatz, Taylor,[16] and William Tiley properties to Braddock Park. About 350 feet north of this park is an old milestone, which is supposed by some writers to have been set up by Braddock.[17] Leaving Braddock Park the line follows the Midlothian road for about four hundred feet; but, soon entering a lane, it crosses the western branch of George's Creek east of an old spring-house standing near the ruins of the old Musselman farmhouse, and bearing the inscription "C. & S. Musselman, May 30th, 1806."[18] At this point, one-fourth mile west from Braddock Park, the ascent of Big Savage Mountain begins. Although there are some level spots on the western slope of the mountain, the ascent of more than two miles is very steep and rocky, and the cut is several feet deep in places.[19] The descent for a half mile or more is also very rugged and in places extraordinarily steep.[20] On the east and west slopes the traces of the route are very distinct.

Lacock's footnote to the first-quoted sentence, *"See Middleton's map"*, suggests that he relied on Middleton's map when he turns the route to the left to follow Flaggy (Preston) Run and describes the route as *"apparently following the west bank of the stream"*. The use of the word *"apparently"* suggests that Lacock could not identify the roadbed at this point. Instead, he describes a *"deep depression formed by an old mill race that might easily be mistaken for the road"*. The third sentence — still referencing Hoffman Hollow — mentions *"an old tramway roadbed which might readily be taken for Braddock's path"*. The fourth sentence mentions *"a very deep scar, which is probably a part of Braddock's roadbed"*. The words in these sentences are not ones that instill or convey confidence.

Unlike the route described by Atkinson and Middleton, Lacock's projected route (Figure 3) takes a sharp right-hand turn at the top of Hoffman Hollow, heading northward along the valley of Georges Creek toward Grahamtown, and ultimately connecting with the traditional route of Braddock's road through Frostburg. Lacock describes and illustrates the second camp as being east of Georges Creek, near the end of a ridge, overlooking Frostburg. Subsequent road historians have followed Lacock's lead concerning the route between Clarysville and Frostburg, illustrating it as passing through Hoffman Hollow and Grahamtown.[21]

---

[16] The Taylor survey is included herein as Figure 37.

[17] Lacock's footnote here is, *"See Lowdermilk's History of Cumberland, 257. This stone, sometimes designated Braddock's Stone, bears the following inscription: '11 mile To F ᵗ Cumberland 29 M ˢ To Cap ᵗⁿ Smyth's Inn and Bridge Big Crossings & The Best Road To Redstone Old Fort 64 M.' This is fairly legible. The other side reads, 'Our countrys rights we will defend.' There is no reason for supposing that this stone was erected by Braddock's command."*

[18] This springhouse is good evidence of the existence of a nearby road in 1806. In Figure 1, the rectangle that is located between two of the red dots (within the grounds of the present-day Frostburg State University Arboretum) may be the referenced springhouse; compare to Figure 32.

[19] Lacock's footnote here is, *"On the summit of the mountain, a few hundred yards to the north of the road, is St. John Rock, 2930 feet above sea level, from which a magnificent view of the surrounding country is to be had."*

[20] Lacock's footnote here is, *"Three wagons were entirely destroyed in passing this mountain, and several more were shattered (Orme Journal, 335)."*

[21] For example, Braddock Road historian Norman L. Baker places Martin's plantation and the second encampment east of Georges Creek. He describes it as being in the vicinity of the eastern part of the Allegany Cemetery and the

This book presents evidence suggesting that the march did not follow the Hoffman Hollow valley west of Clarysville that the National Freeway (Route 68) now follows, and presents evidence suggesting that the second camp was located west of the eastern head fork of Georges Creek.

The second report of the commissioners for the National Road

One document that is harmonious with Lacock's projected route through Hoffman Hollow is found in footnote 12 of his book, and concerns the second report of the commissioners for the National Road. The footnote includes the following statement:

> *In their second report, under date of January 15, 1808, the commissioners show that the new road followed only a very small portion of the Braddock Road. "The law," runs the document, "requiring the commissioners to report those parts of the route as are laid on the old road, as well as those on new grounds, and to state those parts which require the most immediate attention and amelioration, the probable expense of making the same passable in the most difficult parts, and through the whole distance, they have to state that, from the crooked and hilly course of the road now traveled, the new route could not be made to occupy any part of it (except an intersection on Wills Mountain [Sandy Gap], another at Jesse Tomlinson's [Little Meadows], and a third near Big Youghioghana [Somerfield][22], embracing not a mile of distance in the whole) without unnecessary sacrifices of distance and expense" (Executive Document, 10 Cong., 1 sess., Feb. 19, 1808, 8 pp.).*

At first blush, this report seems to completely validate the route Lacock describes through Hoffman Hollow, because there are only two possible valleys to follow westward from Clarysville, and the National Road occupies the valley of Porter Run. The problem with this seemingly obvious interpretation of the report is that east of Clarysville, the National Road and Braddock's road both follow the valley of Braddock Run, nearby to one another.[23] With this fact in mind, it becomes clear that the commissioners are referring to places where the National Road would occupy the exact same ground as the route that was then known as Braddock's road *("laid on the old road")*, rather than referring to places where the two roads were merely situated close to one another. In

---

northeast portion of Grahamtown. See his 2016 book, "**Braddock's Road Historical Atlas**", page 126. Also see related maps on pages 138, 139, and 141 to 144.

[22] Lacock's *"Somerfield"* note is mistaken. Braddock's expedition passed well to the south of Somerfield, traveling along Braddock Run, and forded the Youghiogheny River near the mouth of Braddock Run, as detailed elsewhere herein. (This is not the same Braddock Run that is located east of Clarysville.)

[23] Lacock described the route of Braddock's road along Braddock Run as follows, *"Less than a quarter of a mile west of Charles Laber's house Braddock Road again crosses Braddock Run; thence turning almost due south in order to avoid a rocky ascent over which no road could be built, it comes into the National turnpike about a mile west of the old toll-house. From this point it coincides with the turnpike for 225 feet; then it veers away to the north for some rods and turns west, crossing the county road known as the Short Gap road about fifty yards north of its junction with the turnpike, and passing the house now owned by John Laber. A short distance west of this point it crosses the turnpike and the Eckhart branch of the Cumberland and Pennsylvania Railroad in order to avoid a very deep hollow, and joins the pike again four hundred feet farther on. After following the old turnpike for about one hundred feet it veers away again to the north of it at Spruce Bridge for about three-quarters of a mile, passing Smith's Big Rocks, and joining the turnpike again less than quarter of a mile east of Clarysville. From Alleghany Grove Camp Ground to Clarysville there are only a few short stretches where traces of the road cannot be distinctly seen, and in some places the scar is nearly ten feet deep."* Compare this rich detail to the paucity of information found in Lacock's description of his projected route through Hoffman Hollow.

other words, the report of the commissioners does not rule out the theory that Braddock's expedition followed the valley of Porter Run.

The twin problems faced by Atkinson and Lacock

The first problem faced by Atkinson and Lacock is that they lived at a time when it was difficult to find original documentary evidence. Nowadays, in the year 2017, such evidence is widely disseminated via the internet, and searches can be augmented by crowd sourcing on history websites. The evidence presented in this paper was acquired using these methods.[24]

The second problem faced by Atkinson and Lacock is that their research took place long after Braddock's 1755 march. In the ensuing time, the route westward from Fort Cumberland was improved a number of times prior to the development of the National Road, local transportation needs produced a complex network of roads, and parts of the original route were effaced by more recent activity.

I like to think that Atkinson and Lacock would be flattered if they knew that we continue their research today, tweaking it a bit here and there, using the tools that are now available. I think they would have been thrilled to have access to LIDAR,[25] GPS,[26] satellite imagery, historical aerial photography, all the early maps and surveys that are now available online, metal detectors, and ready access to various interested parties who are willing to share what they know. This book may challenge some of their findings, but it is they who inspired many generations to have an interest in the course of Braddock's march. We owe them a debt of gratitude for their pioneering research activities and their publications.

Henry Temple's article concerning 1908 research that was conducted with Lacock

Lacock's research associate Henry Temple, a Professor of History at Washington and Jefferson College, wrote an article titled *"Braddock's Road"* that was published in the 1908 proceedings of the second annual meeting of the Ohio Valley History Association.[27] Temple wrote:

> *It must be remembered, however, here and elsewhere in this paper identified with the route of General Braddock's army is a mark left by many years' travel on the pioneer road long called by Braddock's name. That it followed everywhere exactly upon Braddock's trace cannot be*

---

[24] Much of the documentary evidence included in this book was identified by members of the Western Maryland History Facebook group. I have used footnotes to acknowledge the individuals who identified the various evidence presented herein, without meaning to imply that they all necessarily endorse my research and conclusions.

[25] The National Oceanic and Atmospheric Administration of the U.S. Department of Commerce describes LIDAR as follows, *"LIDAR, which stands for Light Detection and Ranging, is a remote sensing method that uses light in the form of a pulsed laser to measure ranges (variable distances) to the Earth. These light pulses—combined with other data recorded by the airborne system— generate precise, three-dimensional information about the shape of the Earth and its surface characteristics."*

[26] Global Positioning System. GPS coordinates are expressed in latitude and longitude. The GPS coordinates that are included in this book can be entered into Internet mapping services to locate the referenced sites. Several services allow the user to switch between map, satellite, and topography views. Enter the latitude and longitude coordinates without the degree symbols, separated by a comma, into the map search field. GPS coordinates can also be used in navigation systems to generate directions.

[27] **"Annual Report of the Ohio Valley Historical Association"**, Volume 2.

ascertained. Yet it is not a wholly unwarranted assumption that the early travelers would in general follow that trace rather than cut a new way through the forest.

Descending from Sandy Gap the old road leads to the grove now occupied by the summer cottages and auditorium of the Alleghany Camp Ground. Near this place was General Braddock's first camp, which in his orderly book is called "the camp in the grove," but in Captain Orme's journal it is called "Spendelow Camp." The old road crosses the run at a ford and proceeds westerly three and a half miles to Clarysville, lying most of the way north of the pike and distant from it sometimes only a few yards. At Clarysville the two roads separate and do not touch again for nearly ten miles, the Braddock road passing through a gap at the Hoffman mines, sometimes coinciding with the modern public road and sometimes showing a plain scar through the fields. It passes through the southern outskirts of Frostburg, Maryland. It was in this neighborhood that General Braddock made his second camp, at a place called in Captain Orme's journal "Martin's Plantations." Martin's place is shown on Shippen's draft, of 1759, reproduced in Hulbert's **"Historic Highways."**

The first two sentences of the Temple quote are very much on-point, and should be fully absorbed by anyone studying Braddock's road or any other early primitive road. The third sentence, *"Yet it is not a wholly unwarranted assumption that the early travelers would in general follow that trace rather than cut a new way through the forest"* overlooks the fact that there were government-sponsored road improvements west of Fort Cumberland after Braddock's expedition, during the second half of the eighteenth century. These improvements are referenced later in this book.

Factors that make it difficult to research the route of Braddock's expedition

Evidence exists that Braddock traveled during a very dry period. Washington's June 28, 1755 letter to his brother John mentions that Buffalo River (French Creek) *"must be as dry as we now found the Great Crossing of the Youghiogany, which may be passed dry-shod."* The drought was so bad that Robert H. Morris, *"Lieutenant Governor and Commander in-Chief of the Province of Pennsylvania, and Counties of New Castle, Kent, and Sussex, upon Delaware"*, proclaimed a day of fasting for June 17, 1755. The introduction to the proclamation[28] states, *"There having been no Rain for two or three Months, and all Sorts of Grain near perishing, and as the General was beginning his March, the Governor and Council unanimously thought it necessary to appoint a Fast, Which was done by Proclamation in these Words…"* These drought references indicate that any deeply sunken roads that Atkinson, Lacock, and Temple found were not created solely by the march of Braddock's army — not that any serious researcher would ever think that. The drought references can also be logically interpreted as meaning that the lack of an identifiable rut along Porter Run is not proof that Braddock did not follow Porter Run. In weather so dry, the army could very well have marched up the valley of Porter Run without leaving marks that would still be identifiable back when Atkinson, Lacock and Temple were searching for them.

---

[28] See the minutes of the Provincial Council.

A number of traditions,[29] and various bits of documentary evidence, indicate that Braddock's road was used primarily by packhorse trains for many years after Braddock's expedition.[30] For example, John Bradberry's 1838 Revolutionary War pension application includes the statement, *"...he was engaged in active service as one of a detachment who were employed in packing flour on horses from a place called 'old Fort Cumberland' in said state of Pennsylvania to a Fort a short distance below the junction of the Allegany and Monongahelia Rivers called 'Fort Red Stick' he believes said last mentioned Fort was also in said state of Pennsylvania..."* For another example, on November 5, 1778, Colonel Richard Campbell wrote a letter to Colonel Archibald Steel and Captain Patrick Lockhart from Fort McIntosh that includes the following statement, *"You will Immediately prepare and order all the Horses to be Collected that is fit for service.—You are to have 300 taken out of the number that is fit for service kept for Immediate use at this post, five hundred is to be Immediately sent to Fort Cumberland to bring flour and salt to this post under the Care of Mr Brady."* I am not aware of traces of any packhorse roads that have survived to the present day, although they surely must exist somewhere on this broad continent. If it was indeed primarily packhorse traffic that followed the hypothetical route of Braddock's road up Porter Run, and that portion of the route eventually transitioned to Hoffman Hollow, I doubt that there would have been much of anything left for Atkinson, Lacock and Temple to identify as the sunken wagon road they were looking for.

It would certainly come as no surprise to anyone who studies early North American transportation that an early packhorse path may have followed Hoffman Hollow, or that such a path followed an even earlier Indian path. It would also come as no surprise that such a hypothetical packhorse route eventually morphed into a sunken road that became eroded long after Braddock's march by the wagons of local farmers and countless westward migrating settlers. The mere fact that wagon traffic, occurring long after Braddock's expedition, produced a sunken road somewhere — Hoffman Hollow, for example — is not evidence that the sunken road represents the original course of Braddock's military road.

I performed a very thorough study of the Turkey Foot Road that was opened westward from Fort Cumberland in 1779 to supply Fort Pitt. During that study, I found a number of route variations, sometimes separated by significant distance, that were all contemporaneously known as the Turkey Foot Road. For example, see the route shown on 1785 Joseph Francis survey and the John Halteman *"Camp Misery"* survey, compared to the parallel route shown on the 1819 Adam Fehdle (Faidley) survey.[31] From that intensive road study, I became aware that primitive roads sometimes experienced significant route variations over time that all carried the same name. I also learned that I couldn't always find traces of the old road. In one case, this even occurred in a constricted

---

[29] As an example of one of various sources of packhorse traditions, Jacob Brown's 1896 book "**Brown's Miscellaneous Writings...**" indicates that packhorses were the norm on Braddock's road for many years, stating, *"This now historic road, when made, was of sufficient capacity to pass vehicles; with a mere removal of timber and rocks—no engineering, grading, or smoothing. But there was scarcely a wagon passed over it for the first thirty years. Such heavy articles as salt, iron, etc., were carried from the East to the West over the mountains on pack horses. Tradition (the oldest inhabitant cannot reach back) tells how they then went in convoys, single file, in this road."*

[30] For various other examples, see the book "**Fort Cumberland: The missing years**", Dietle, 2016.

[31] For these surveys, see "**In Search of the Turkey Foot Road**", fourth edition, Dietle & McKenzie, 2014.

and relatively undisturbed valley. When I look at the 1898 topographical map included herein as Figure 1, and see the National Road, two railroads,[32] a village, and a number of other structures in the valley of Porter Run, I don't find it too surprising that there would be no remaining trace of a primitive road there today, or during Lacock's early 1900s study.

During my study of the Turkey Foot Road, there were only a few places where I could definitively say, *"this is the original military route cut in 1779"*, or even say *"this is probably the original military route"*. There were just too many route variations over time. Where I could make such statements, it was due to exceptionally early surveys that reference the road, or exceptionally constricted terrain. For example, in the Jennings Run water gap there is a place where a rock cliff was located ten or fifteen feet from the original natural course of Jennings Run, and the original military road simply had to pass through those few feet of ground. It would be pure folly of me to say that some particular and well-proven route variation represents the original 1779 military route, based solely on its sunken depth or the mere existence of that route variation, even if I could prove it was already long-abandoned in the mid-1800s. It seems like an even greater folly for Atkinson to declare, without even so much as a contemporaneous survey naming the road, that a particular sunken road that just happened to be located in a plausible location represents the route of Braddock's army. If all the other evidence herein pointing to Porter Run is ignored, or can adequately be explained away, Atkinson's projected route still only has a 50:50 chance of even being in the right valley.

Comparing the route options

One thing in favor of Atkinson's projected route via Hoffman Hollow is that it isn't as steep as that portion of the route of the National Road that is located between the village of Eckhart Mines and Frostburg. This advantage is confirmed by the topographical map that is included herein as Figure 1. This advantage, however, could also explain why the route via Hoffman Hollow eventually became popular enough to produce a sunken wagon road. A disadvantage of Atkinson's projected route is that it crosses over higher terrain, compared to the terrain between the village of Eckhart Mines and Frostburg. This too is apparent from Figure 1.

One of the main arguments against the Porter Run theory is that the terrain crossed by the Hoffman Hollow route is not as steep — even though Orme described the route between the first and second camps as *"excessively mountainous and rocky"*. Orme's statement actually fits the Porter Run theory fairly well. The projected route certainly includes some steep terrain, and an 1884 photo by Thomas Dwight Biscoe[33] shows the Porter Run valley just above Clary's tavern as being quite narrow and rocky.

Atkinson informed us that terrain wasn't always the deciding factor, when he wondered why Braddock's engineers didn't follow the more favorable course of the National Road over Savage Mountain. There are deeper mysteries than this to be found in the courses selected for 1700s roads.

---

[32] Patrick H. Stakem's book "**Eckhart Mines, The National Road, & the Eckhart Railroad**" indicates that the Eckhart railroad was completed in 1846, and the Hoffman branch railroad was built in 1859.

[33] Thomas Dwight Biscoe Collection, Marietta College, identified by Scott Williams.

Why, for example, did the Turkey Foot Road go straight up and down the over the formidably steep flanks of the Allegheny Mountain, instead of detouring slightly to follow the Greenville Gap,[34] avoiding the mountain altogether? Directness sometimes took precedence over more favorable terrain. This helps to explain why people took the Colonial Road (described later herein) over Haystack Mountain, wearing it into a deep rut (which Lacock mistakenly thought was Braddock's original military road) instead of going through the Narrows water gap.

Dave Williams grew up in a log cabin on the western edge of Clarysville in the 1950s and 1960s. Having walked both ways to Frostburg many times, he views the route through the village of Eckhart Mines as being preferable to taking Hoffman Hollow. He wrote, *"The hike from Clarysville to Frostburg via Eckhart is far from daunting. Our mother walked it daily for years, as she never drove a car. ... In contrast, the walk up Hoffman Hollow is definitely the long way around the barn..."*

Referring to Figure 1 and Figure 4, one can readily see that the route projected by this book, via the village of Eckhart Mines, would be less circuitous that Lacock's projected route through Hoffman Hollow.[35] More specifically, the route via Eckhart Mines would be on the order of about 0.78-miles shorter than the route via Hoffman Hollow, which makes the route via Hoffman Hollow about 38% longer than the route via Eckhart Mines. This makes no significant difference in an automobile, but after a person has found many shortcut routes across the mountains, as I have, one begins to realize that distance was an important factor in the days of horse powered transportation.

A book by Robert Bruce helps to solidify the consensus route

In 1916, Robert Bruce published a well-known book titled "**The National Road**" that was written with the assistance of John Kennedy Lacock. A map (Figure 4) in Bruce's book provides a detailed look at Lacock's projected route of Braddock's road through Hoffman Hollow, and on to Grahamtown, and also identifies Lacock's projected location of Braddock's second encampment. Over the years, the detailed route shown in Bruce's book has become the consensus route of Braddock's expedition between Clarysville and Frostburg; i.e., the conventional wisdom. Likewise, Lacock's projected location of the second camp has also become the accepted conventional wisdom.

---

[34] The Greenville Gap was formed by Piney Run and Little Piney Run, and separates Allegheny Mountain from Meadow Mountain near Salisbury, Pennsylvania.
[35] This comparative route length observation was made by Dave Williams.

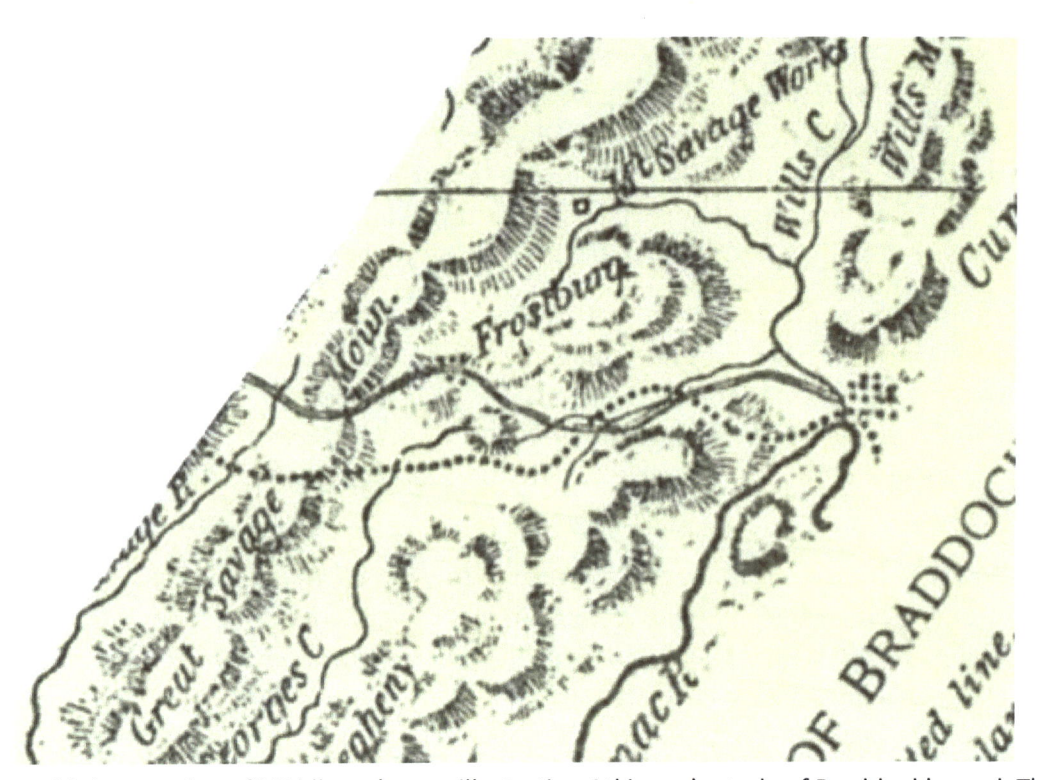

Figure 2 — This is a portion of Middleton's map illustrating Atkinson's study of Braddock's road. This map depicts Braddock's route as passing south of the hill that is located just west of Clarysville (i.e., along Preston Run and Hoffman Hollow), and does not depict the route as turning north toward Grahamtown and Frostburg after the hill. Although this is not a precisely drawn map, Atkinson wrote, *"Passing then a mile to the South of Frostburg, the road approaches the East foot of Savage Mountain, which it crosses about one mile South of the National Road..."* The *"a mile to the South of Frostburg"* statement indicates that Atkinson was referring to a road that was well to the south of the traditional route of Braddock's road through the Frostburg area.

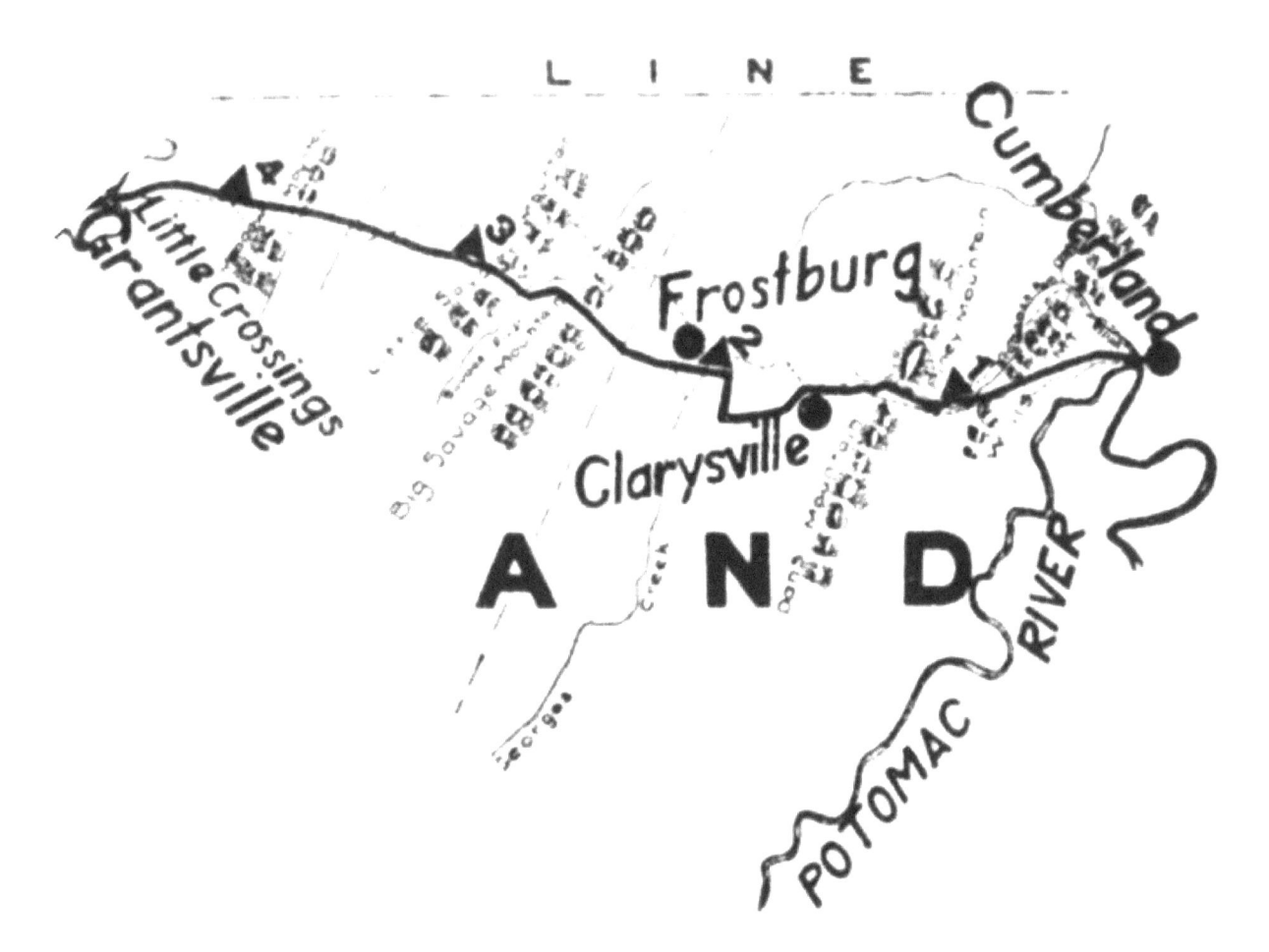

Figure 3 — This is a portion of Lacock's published map of Braddock's road. It shows the road passing through Hoffman Hollow, and then making a sharp right-hand turn northward toward Grahamtown, following the valley of Georges Creek. It positions the second camp eastward of the eastern head fork of Georges Creek. Lacock's map documents the traditional route of Braddock's road through Frostburg, where it crosses both head forks of Georges Creek.

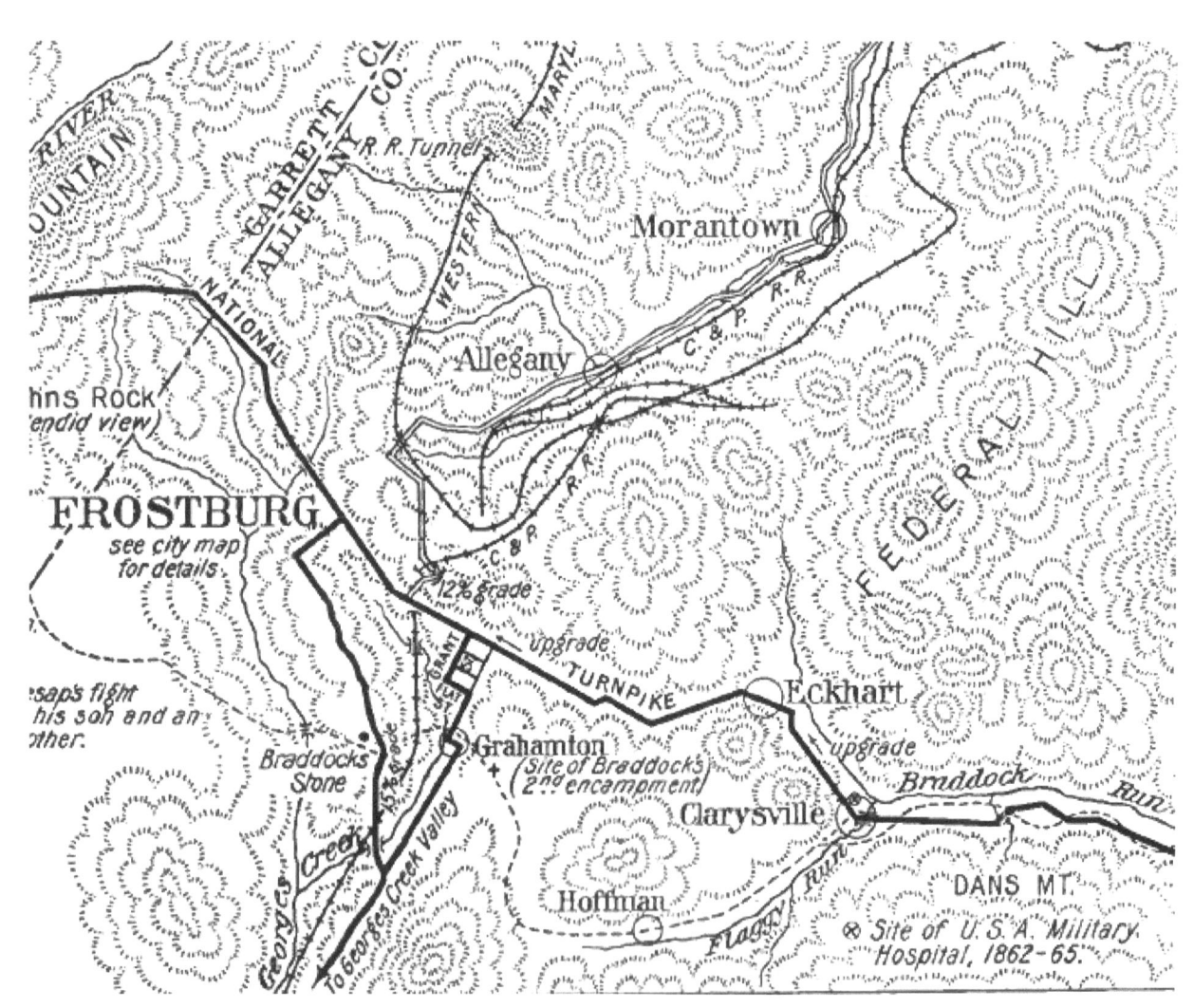

Figure 4 — This is from a map that is included in Robert Bruce's 1916 book "**The National Road**". The book was created with the help of John Kennedy Lacock, and this map provides much more detail concerning Lacock's projected route of Braddock's road between Clarysville and Frostburg, compared to the map in Lacock's book "**Braddock Road**". This map is the basis for the current consensus route of Braddock's expedition between Clarysville and Frostburg, and is the basis for the current consensus location of Braddock's second encampment. It portrays Braddock's route as taking a hard right-hand turn up the valley of Georges Creek after reaching the top of Hoffman Hollow.

3. Post-1755 improvements to Braddock's road

Introduction

This chapter describes a number of government-authorized repairs of, and potential alterations to, Braddock's road long before Atkinson's study. These road improvement activities help to illustrate why it is difficult to determine the original military route.

1758 road repairs by Major Peachey

On July 10, 1758, Bouquet wrote a letter to Pitt that includes the statement, *"For were I to pursue Mr Braddock's route, I should save but little labour, as that road is now a brush wood, by the sprouts from the old stumps, which must be cut down and made proper for Carriages as well as any other passage that we must attempt."* Washington expressed a different opinion, which was colored by his desire that Forbes' army follow a route that would benefit his home state of Virginia.[36] On July 16, 1758 he wrote a letter to Bouquet that includes the statement, *"I shall direct the officer, that marches out, to take particular pains in reconnoitering General Braddock's road, though I have had repeated information that it only wants such small repairs, as could with ease be made as fast as the army would march."* On July 21, 1758, Washington wrote another letter that included the statement, *"...tomorrow Major Peachey, with three hundred men, will proceed to open General Braddock's road. I shall direct them to go to George's Creek, ten miles in advance."* On July 25, 1758, Washington wrote another letter that includes the statement, *"Major Peachey, who commands the working party on Braddock's road, writes to me, that he finds few repairs wanting."*[37]

1759 road improvements

A July 22, 1759 letter Tulleken wrote to Bouquet includes the following statement:

> *As to opening the Communication between Ft. Cumberland and Pittsburgh it would certainly be of infinite service and is much to be wish'd for; Col. Byrd had received your orders on that head,*

---

[36] On July 23, 1758, James Young, commissary of musters and paymaster general, wrote to Richard Peters that *"The Virginians are making great interest that our Rout may be by Cumberland, but I hope they will not succeed."* On August 9, 1758, Forbes wrote a letter to Bouquet that stated *"By a very unguarded letter of Col. Washington that accidentally fell into my hands, I am now at the bottom of their scheme against this new road, a scheme that I think was a shame for any officer to be concerned in, but more of this at meeting."* On September 2, 1758, Washington wrote a letter to the Lieutenant Governor of Virginia that included the statement *"In the conference I had with Colo. Bouquet ... I did among other things to avert the resolve of opening a new Road, represent the great Expence the Coloney of Virg'a had been at to support the War ... and after this demonstrated very clearly the time it wou'd take us to proceed on the old Road; and at how much easier expence, even if we were oblig'd to get all our provisions and Stores from Pensylvania; and no occasion for this surely. In fine I urg'd every thing then I could do now ... but urg'd in vain, the Pensylvanians whose Interest present and future it was to conduct the Expedition thro' their Government, and along that way, because it secures their Frontiers at present, and the Trade hereafter ..."* On September 4, 1758, Forbes wrote *"Therefore would consult G. Washington, although perhaps not follow his advice, as his Behavior about the roads, was in no ways like a soldier."* On October 3, 1758, Colonel John Armstrong wrote to Peters *"The Virginians are much chagrined at the opening of the road through this government, and Colonel Washington has been a good deal sanguine and obstinate upon the occasion."* Also see Volume 2, page 22 of the 1906 book "**History of Bedford and Somerset Counties...**"

[37] These four letters are quoted from Archer Butler Hubert's 1903 book "**The Old Glade (Forbes's) Road (Pennsylvania State Road)**".

but...Col. Byrd not thinking one hundred men sufficient for that end, and likewise imagining as things then stood that you would want all his people this way he has done nothing in it, and hopes the General will approve of his measures.

A synopsis of an August 2, 1759 letter Alexander Finnie wrote to Tulleken from Fort Cumberland states, *"Sends returns; will begin to work on the road with a working party, so as to get one day's start of the waggons. There are here 64 waggons 500 sheep and some cattle; does not know to whom they all belong."*

A synopsis of an August 3, 1759 letter Bouquet wrote from Fort Bedford states, *"The same[38] to the officer at Fort Cumberland. That the cattle coming from Virginia to the westward are to be appraised. All provisions from Virginia or Maryland are to take Braddock's road."*

Burd's journal states, *"Ordered in August, 1759, to march with two hundred men of my battalion to the mouth of Redstone Creek, where it empties itself into the river Monongahela, to cut a road somewhere from Gen. Braddock's road to that place..."* This is included so the reader understands where Burd was heading as the following correspondence was being written.

On September 4, 1759 letter Bouquet sent a letter[39] to Colonel Burd from Bedford that includes the statement, *"... I have a mind to employ the 30 new Waggons from Hambright to carry between Cumberland & Redstone Creek, The distance will be shorter, The Road they Say better and the grass certainly So; But of this I Shall be glad to have your sentiment; and to know for certain what sort of Road you will find."*

A synopsis[40] of a September 5, 1759 letter Colonel Burd wrote to Bouquet from the *"Camp at Martin's"* states, *"Has only got this length (ten miles from Fort Cumberland) owing to the heavy rain. From Cumberland the road is hilly and stony, and in the short distance they have crossed 14 or 15 creeks, not a single bridge repaired and very little done on the road."*[41]

A letter[42] Colonel Burd wrote to Bouquet from *"Camp at the Little Meadows, Sept. 7th, 1759"* includes the following statement:

The road from my last encampment to this is really excessively bad; the Alleghany Hill is by no means the worst of it; there are two hills extremely bad and long. From Martin's place to this they esteem it eleven miles, and I think it very bad for wagons. There has been nothing done upon it by Finney. If the road is all along as I have found it hither, I think wagons can carry one-third more on the other roads than this, and with more ease to the horses; and I would strongly advise that a party from Fort Cumberland may be ordered upon this road from thence to Guest's;

---

[38] Bouquet.
[39] **"The Pennsylvania Magazine of History and Biography"**, Volume 33, 1909.
[40] **"Sessional Papers of the Parliament of the Dominion of Canada"**, Volume 23, Issue 6.
[41] With this passage in mind, it isn't too difficult to imagine improvised detours developing to bypass faulty bridges across unavoidable ravines. Colonel William Eyer's 1762 journal also states that the bridges were out of repair, and mentions the bad condition and rockiness of the road, and states that a number of trees were fallen across the road. (**"Western Pennsylvania History Magazine"**, XXVII.)
[42] **"Letters and Papers Relating Chiefly to the Provincial History of Pennsylvania"**, 1855.

I'll answer[43] from thence to the mouth of Redstone Creek, The commanding officer of the party should not hurry, but make the road good, and take time. It seems to me that Mr. Braddock was in a hurry to get along, and so did not allow time to make the road as it ought or easily could be made. It is not more than ten feet wide, and carried right up every hill almost without a turn, and the hills almost perpendicular; however, if the officer who is sent on it from Cumberland has any understanding and regard for the service, he may make it a good communication, as it is very capable of improvement; and I know I could make it a good road for the part of the country, but as it now stands it is too bad. You know Mr. Avery weighed the loads of my wagons, and they were 12 cwt. I found they could not get along even with this moderate load; and I took out about 14 cwt. and loaded upon the officers' horses, and at the hill I put six soldiers to each wagon to hoist them up. I hope to march from hence twelve miles to-day; if I make out this march I will be very happy at night. I observe you have some thought of sending the three wagons this way. I hope they will do very well after the road is mended; as the hills must be turned up by winding, and not left as they are now, straight up. The stones must be thrown out of the road, all new bridges, and old ones tossed on one side, and I think the road should be widened; but this might be dispensed with. I am very glad the General will find a conveyance to meet me at the Monongahela. I will immediately upon my arrival ascertain the situation of the water, and then we can proceed accordingly with the transportation from Cumberland. The weather has been very severe upon my people, and not a little so upon myself, as I have had a fever; but now we are all in good spirits and no complaints.

In this letter to Bouquet, Burd is clearly recommending route alterations.

A September 13, 1759 letter[44] Bouquet wrote to Burd includes the following statement:

I received your favours of the 5th & 7th Instant and hope you have got to your ground by this time, The weather having been remarkably fine. ... Had we Tools and proper People to employ, the reparation of Braddocks Road would be very necessary; for want of those two things, I am afraid we shall do nothing Cap[t] Pearis has orders to join you with his Company, taking the Pack Horses under his Escort, and Lieut. Jones is to follow with the next Convoy to you.

A synopsis[45] of a November 27, 1759 letter Bouquet wrote from Fort Cumberland states *"to Capt. Richard Paris, at Cumberland Fort, instructing him to open a new road, to repair damages, &c."* Whether this relates to opening a new road heading westward Fort Cumberland is unknown, but seems possible considering Burd's September 5, 1759 and September 7, 1759 letters and Bouquet's September 13, 1759 letter. The phrases *"repair damages"* and *"open a new road"* may suggest repairing an existing road, and making route improvements when warranted. A 1760 survey, presented later in this book, describes a route then-known as Braddock's road that was 710 yards west of the western end of Hoffman Hollow, and aligned with Hoffman Hollow, over a mile south of the traditional route of Braddock's road through Frostburg. Which is the original route and which is a dramatic alteration? There are clues. One clue is a 1753 survey presented later in

---

[43] Burd apparently means that he will be responsible for the condition of that part of the route.
[44] "**The Pennsylvania Magazine of History and Biography**", Volume 33, 1909.
[45] "**Sessional Papers of the Parliament of the Dominion of Canada**", Volume 23, Issue 6.

this book, and a map by George Washington, that put the route of Nemacolin's Ohio Company road a mile away from of Hoffman Hollow. Another clue is the detail found on the *"Gordon map"*, which is also presented later in this book.

1766 road improvements

Although not documentary evidence, the 1910 book "**History of Harrison County, West Virginia**" states that in November 1766, the Virginia Assembly appointed commissioners *"To view, lay out and direct a road to be cleared from the North branch of the Potomac to Fort Pitt on the Ohio, by or near the road called Braddock's road, in the most direct and cheapest manner the said commissioners think fit, and two hundred pounds were appropriated for that purpose."* The November 7, 1766 act is recorded in "**Hening's Statutes at Large**", and states:

> *I. Whereas it is represented to this present general assembly, that by opening a road from the frontiers of this colony to Fort Pitt on the Ohio, a very advantageous trade might be carried on with the Indians, in alliance with the British crown on the western frontiers of this dominion, and the king's garrisons be better supplied with provisions; Be it therefore enacted by the Lieutenant-Governor, Council and Burgesses of this present General Assembly, and it is hereby enacted by the authority of the same, That Thomas Walker, Thomas Rutherford, James Wood, and Abraham Kite, gentlemen, or any two of them, are hereby appointed, authorized and impowered, to view, lay out, and direct, a road to be cleared from the north branch of Potowmack river to Fort Pitt on the Ohio, by or near the road called Braddock's road, in the most direct and cheapest manner the said commissioners shall think fit. Road to be opened from the north branch of Potowmac to Fort Pitt.*
>
> *II. And be it further enacted by the authority aforesaid, That the treasurer of this colony for the time being is hereby authorized and required to pay to the said commissioners a sum of money not exceeding two hundred pounds in the whole, in such proportions, and at such times, as the said commissioners shall require, to be applied by them towards clearing a road as aforesaid, and the said commissioners shall account for the same to the next general assembly.*

1773 road improvements

A 1773 Maryland act[46] states:

> *And be it enacted that of the said Eighty Thousand Dollars to be emitted in Virtue of this Act such Number as shall be necessary not exceeding Eight thousand Dollars be and are hereby appropriated to be laid out and expended in the cutting clearing amending and putting in good Order a Waggon Road from Fort Cumberland to the nearest Battoc [bateau] navigable Water on the Western side of the Allegany Mountain and the said Eight Thousand Dollars or such part thereof as may be necessary shall and may be laid out and expended in the Work aforesaid by M.ʳ Thomas Johnson Jun.ʳ M.ʳ Henry Griffith M.ʳ Charles Beatty M.ʳ Thomas Sprigg Wootton*

---

[46] This is from the *"Assembly Proceedings, November 16-December 23, 1773"* section of "**Proceedings and Acts of the General Assembly, October 1773 to April 1774**", Volume 64.

Mr Joseph Sprigg Mr Thomas Price and Mr Jonathan Hagar or the Major Part of them who are hereby appointed Supervisors of the said Road and the said Commissioners shall from time to time pay to the Order or Orders of the said Supervisors or the major Part of them any Part or Parts of the said Eight thousand Dollars for the purpose aforesaid of the Expenditure whereof the said Supervis"

This provides another instance where the route may have been *"amended"* west of Clarysville.

The road was in bad shape during the 1779 to 1784 timeframe

A letter Colonel George Morgan wrote to the General Assembly of Pennsylvania on March 25, 1779 includes the statement, *"That great impediments have arisen in the Transportation of public stores to the Ohio, from the badness of the Roads leading to Fort Pitt, which have been neglected so much that Carriages pass with the utmost Difficulty…"* The subject of the letter was a new road Morgan was having opened From Fort Cumberland to supply Fort Pitt via what is now Corriganville and Barrelville — the Turkey Foot Road that I spent many years studying.

Washington's September 10, 1784 journal entry, Andrew Ellicott's November 24, 1784 journal entry, and Doctor Wellford's October 24, 1794 journal entry also describe the bad condition of the road. Washington's September 10, 1784 journal entry includes the statement:

> *The Road from the Old Town to Fort Cumberland we found tolerably good, as it also was from the latter to Gwins,[47] except the Mountain which was pretty long (tho' not steep) in the assent and discent; but from Gwins to Tumberson's it is intolerably bad—there being many steep pinches of the Mountain—deep & miry places and very stony ground to pass over.*

It would be no great surprise if the poor condition of Braddock's road caused travelers to detour around difficult sections of Braddock's road using local roads, where such roads where available. It would also be no great surprise if the poor condition of Braddock's road spurred alternate route development here and there along the course of the road, on both formal and informal bases. Such alterations certainly occurred on other early roads. At present, it appears to be impossible to prove that Lacock's route via Hoffman Hollow isn't just such an alteration, or to prove that it isn't simply a convenient local road that some travelers used to avoid the steep climb out of the valley of Porter Run. Proof that Hoffman Hollow was followed by Braddock's army is sorely lacking. At the same time, some evidence suggesting that Braddock's expedition followed Porter Run does exist. This evidence is the focus of this book.

---

[47] William Brown's 1790 memo book mentions Gwynn's Tavern as follows, *"Gwyns Tavern at the fork, Bradfords old Road"* (Braddock's name was frequently misspelled in the early records). Gwynn's tavern was located where the Winchester Road via Short Gap forked from Braddock's road. The locations of Gwynn's *("Quinns")* and Tomlinson's taverns are shown on the 1792 Reading Howell map of Pennsylvania.

A new road westward from Cumberland is authorized in 1793

Chapter LXX of the 1793 Acts of Maryland states:

WHEREAS the state of Pennsylvania hath laid out, opened and amended, a road from Uniontown, in Fayette county, to the division line:

And whereas the said road will be of no benefit unless this state straighten and amend the road from the town of Cumberland to intersect the said road at the Winding-Ridge; and it appearing to this general assembly that the same will be of considerable advantage to this state, by opening a better communication with the Western country; therefore, Be it enacted, by the General Assembly of Maryland, That George Dent, William M'Mahon and Evan Gwynne, or any two of them, be and they are hereby appointed commissioners, to survey, straighten and amend, at the expence of those who have or may subscribe to the same, a road not exceeding forty feet in width, in the best and most convenient direction from the town of Cumberland, in Allegany county, to a tract of land called Good Will,[48] and from thence to intersect the main road from Union-town, in the state of Pennsylvania, where the said road enters this state at the Winding-Ridge; and the said road, when so opened at the expence of the persons aforesaid, and the valuation herein after directed to be made shall be paid, or secured to be paid, to the individuals concerned, shall be recorded among the records of Allegany county, and be thereafter deemed and taken to be a public road for ever.

This is yet another instance where road construction was authorized westward from Cumberland. Considering all the roadwork that was authorized in the 1700s, after Braddock's expedition, it is no wonder that mistakes have occurred regarding the route of Braddock's expedition. Some of these mistakes are outlined in the following chapter.

---

[48] The *"Good Will"* tract is included on Veatch's map of the Deakins survey of lots west of Fort Cumberland.

4. Alterations that became known as Braddock's road

A colonial road that Lacock mistook for Braddock's road

One alteration to Braddock's road can still be seen along Sandy Gap, where two parallel sunken roads exist. One is currently believed to be Braddock's original route based on artifact discoveries,[49] and the other is believed to be a subsequent alteration. The route Lacock believed to be Braddock's road is now referred to by Braddock Road historians as the *"Colonial Road"*.[50] Both of these roads are located north of and above[51] the present-day road known as Braddock Road (MD 49). The route that is now believed to be Braddock's original route, based on artifact discoveries, is located north of the Colonial Road, and begins at the western end of Camden Avenue. These roads cross one another at latitude 39.642°, longitude -78.808°, and drop down to the present-day Braddock Road (MD 49) at latitude 39.642°, longitude -78.811°. The present-day Braddock Road (MD 49) is a good example of how a more recent alignment of an old road sometimes bears the name of the original route.

The aforementioned post-1755 road improvements[52], and normal local road development, would have made it very difficult for Atkinson and Lacock to accurately delineate the specific route of Braddock's march between Clarysville and Frostburg using on-the-ground studies. This is further complicated by the fact that cases are known where extreme alterations to Braddock's road ultimately became known as Braddock's road.

---

[49] The artifact discoveries that identify one of the roads as an early military road were reported by Robert L. Bantz.
[50] For example, see a discussion of this topic in Norman L. Baker's 2013 book, **"Braddock's Road: Mapping the British Expedition..."**
[51] One reason Braddock's road and the Colonial Road are located so high on the hillside through Sandy Gap is to avoid the most difficult portions of ravines. One of these roads is illustrated as a trail on the 1898 topographical map of the area. (The presence of the trail on the map was identified by Chad Paul.)
[52] While not documentary evidence, the 1906 book **"History of Bedford and Somerset Counties..."** describes a successor to Braddock's road that preceded the National Road:

> In the minds of most people the idea has found place that the "National Road," or pike, as it is more generally known, was laid out over the same ground that the "Braddock road" was. This, however, is a mistake. The Braddock road may be said to have already had a successor before the coming of the pike in a newer road that crossed the Youghiogheny river some distance north of Somerfield, while the crossing place of the Braddock road is south of that village, and is the original "Great Crossing." The crossing place of the "National Road" is at Somerfield, and therefore it is between the other two roads at their several places of crossing the river. This newer road, which was between it and the "National Road," (sic) is usually spoken of as the "Old Road," and was the one that was usually traveled through that part of the country. It is not supposed that this old road was anything more than a common dirt road that in wet weather would be cut up by the wheels of the wagons passing over it, so as to be at times almost impassable. At some places it may have passed over the same ground as the Braddock road, while at other places it crossed it.

> The same may be said of its successor, the "National Road," which at some places is also on the Braddock road, but at others crosses and recrosses it. At places these roads are close together, while at others the "National road" is as much as several miles distant from the Braddock road. What is to be understood is, that the routes of the National, Braddock, and the Old road are the same in direction, but that in most places they are not on precisely the same ground. There are also those who, being more or less familiar with the exact locations of these roads, go so far as to say that at many places both the Braddock and the Old Road had easier grades than those of the "National Road."

The alteration near Mount Pleasant, Pennsylvania

For one example of an extreme alteration, see the very direct route of Braddock's road between Jacobs Creek and Mount Pleasant, Pennsylvania that is illustrated on Barker's 1857 "**Map of Westmoreland Co., Pennsylvania**" (Figure 5)[53], and compare it to the winding route of Braddock's expedition that is described by modern researchers.[54]

An alteration through Petersburg that Lacock mistook as the original route

For another example of an extreme alteration, Walker's 1860 "**Map of Somerset County, Pa**" (Figure 6) illustrates the *"Braddock Route"* as passing just north of Petersburg (now Addison), but Braddock's expedition actually followed Braddock Run, a goodly way to the south. The route alteration shown on the Walker map was already known as *"Braddock's old road"* by 1825, as evidenced by the Zer Hagan survey (Figure 7) at the eastern edge of Petersburg. Lacock mistakenly believed this alteration was the original military route. The mistake was corrected through the 1990s research of Robert L. Bantz, using the *"Gordon map"* (Figure 8)[55], Gordon's journal, the 1788 Conrad Wable survey (Figure 9), and on-the-ground studies. The route along Braddock Run that was documented by Mr. Bantz has become the currently accepted route of Braddock's expedition.[56] This book, relying heavily on the *"Gordon map"*, theorizes that Lacock was also mistaken about the route of Braddock's expedition between Clarysville and Frostburg.

Lacock references the fallibility of tradition

In his book, Lacock obliquely references the difficulty of determining the original route of Braddock's expedition, stating, *"Although many misstatements and untenable notions as to the location of the road, the places of encampment, etc., are prevalent in the country adjacent to the line of march, yet local tradition is in many cases surprisingly accurate."* I had similar experiences while researching the Turkey Foot Road. For example, I encountered one abandoned road that was definitely known locally as the Turkey Foot Road. It ran generally south along the eastern flank of the Allegheny Mountain and crossed over the westerly-running verifiable[57] through-route of the 1700s Turkey Foot Road. This abandoned road probably received its name because the local farmers who lived on the eastern flank of the Allegheny Mountain could follow it to the Greenville Road, passing through the Greenville water gap and on to Confluence, as a shortcut to Mountain Road. This abandoned road is an interesting linear historical feature that crossed the birthplace of my grandfather, but it has nothing to do with the 1700s road I was researching. On the other hand, I encountered people in Somerset and Fayette counties, Pennsylvania who knew exactly where the verifiable 1700s route of the Turkey Foot Road was located. Local tradition is sometimes extremely good, but always has to be carefully evaluated.

---

[53] The route on the Barker map was brought to my attention by Al Wilson.
[54] For example, see the map on page 218 of Norman Baker's 2016 book "**Braddock's Road Historical Atlas**".
[55] Map provided by Robert L. Bantz.
[56] For example, see the map on page 171 of Norman Baker's 2016 book "**Braddock's Road Historical Atlas**".
[57] Unlike in western Maryland, the earliest property surveys in western Pennsylvania frequently illustrate roads and waterways, as a way of identifying the location of the surveyed property.

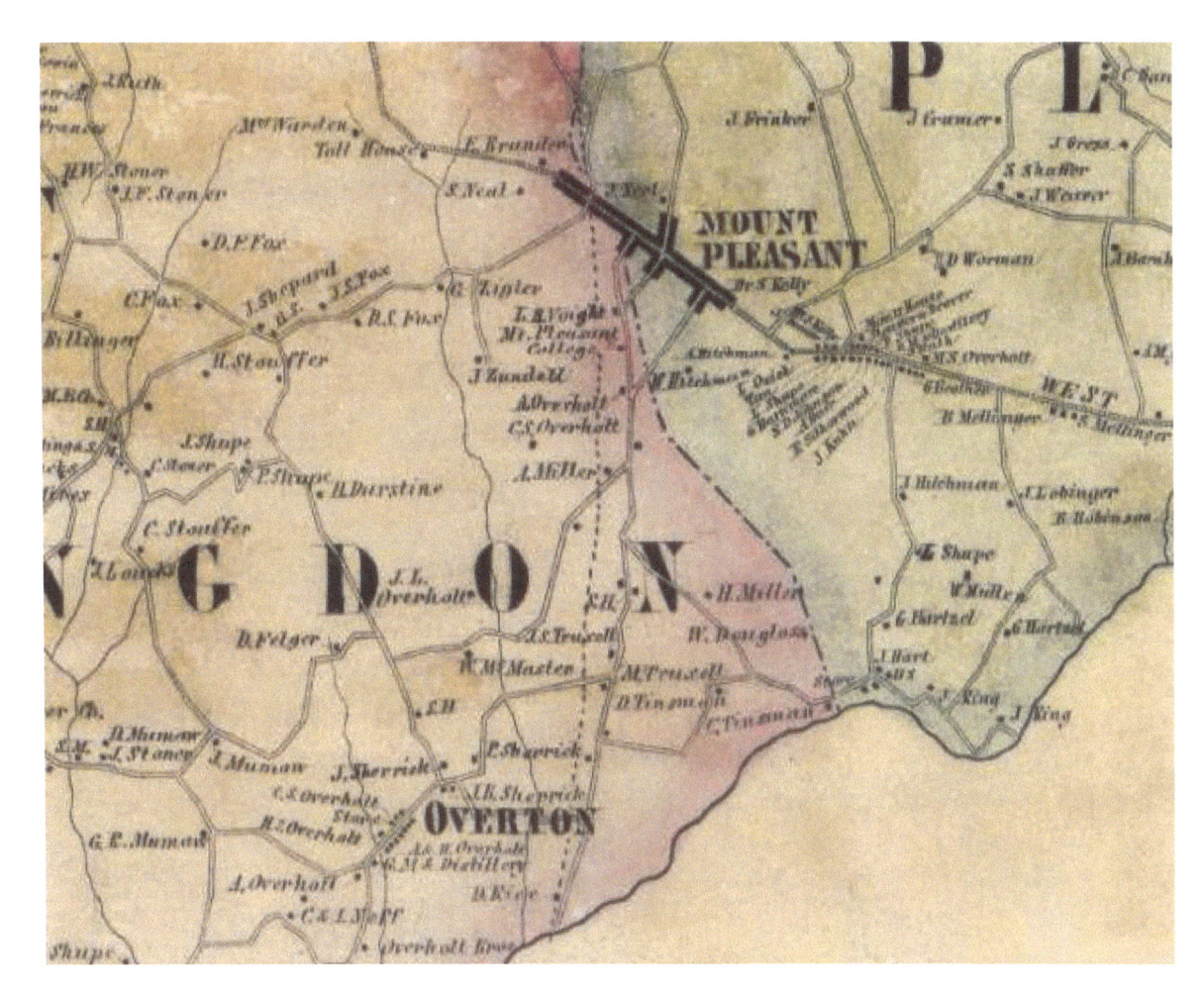

Figure 5 — This is from Barker's 1857 "**Map of Westmoreland Co., Pennsylvania**" (Library of Congress Call No. G3823.W5 1857 .L3). The nearly vertical dashed line in the center of this image is labeled *"Braddock's Road"* elsewhere on the map, but most of the portion of the dashed line shown here is far to the west of the winding route of Braddock's march. In this area, the dashed line represents a shortcut to Braddock's road that uses a good Jacobs Creek fording site (i.e., not swampy) that is located about 1.6-miles from Braddock's fording site, which was at or near Tinsman's (near the township line). As an excellent shortcut to a winding through route, the dashed line route ultimately took on the name of the antecedent through route: Braddock's road.

Figure 6 — This is from Walker's 1860 "**Map of Somerset County, Pa.**" (Library of Congress Call No. G3823.S6 1860 .W3). It illustrates the *"Braddock Route"* as passing through just north of Petersburg, whereas Braddock's expedition actually followed Braddock's Run. This is an example of a dramatic alteration to Braddock's road bearing the name of the antecedent route.

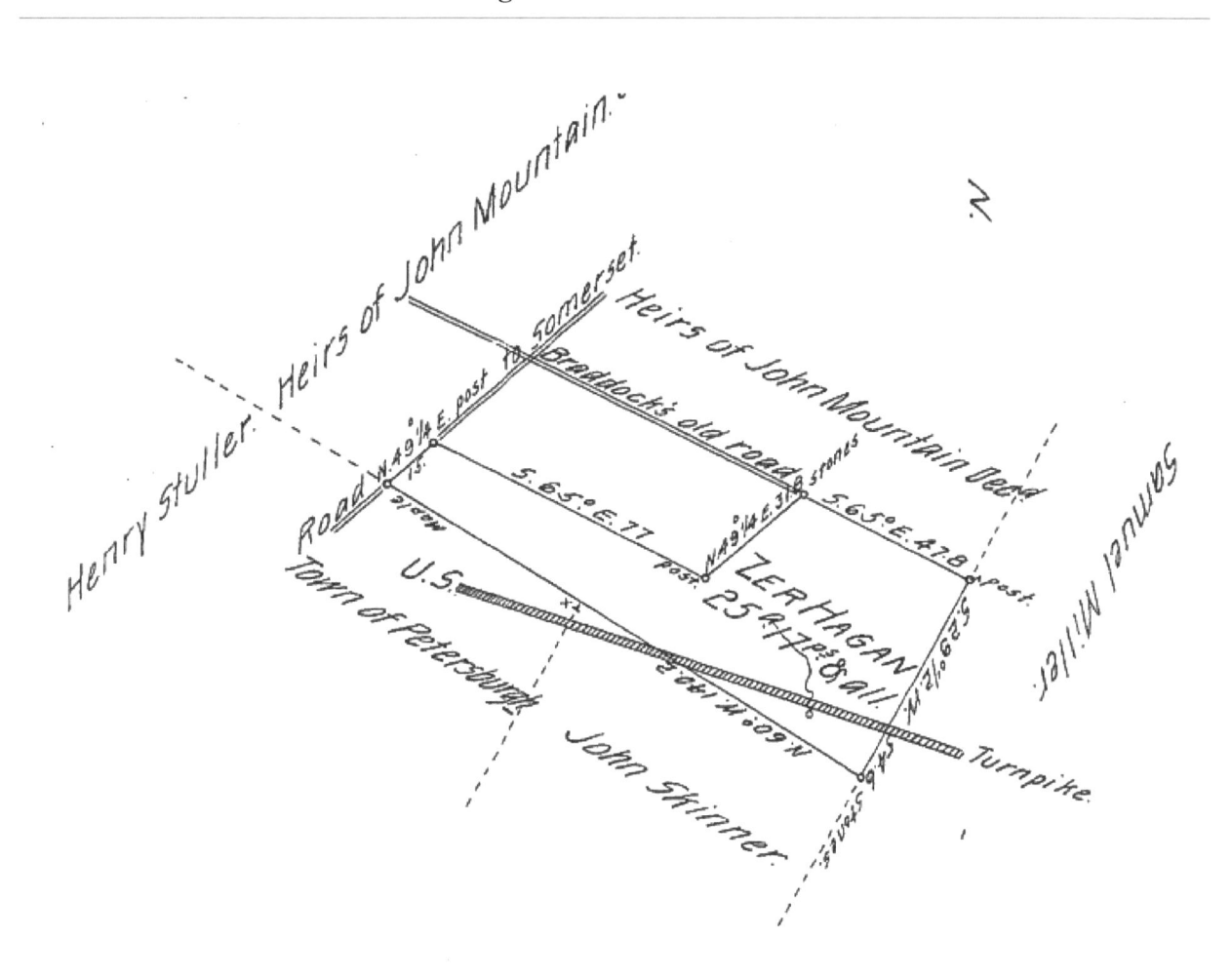

Figure 7 — The 1825 Zer Hagan survey shows that a radical alteration to Braddock's road was already known as *"Braddock's old road"* in 1825 (Survey Book C-90, Page 185).

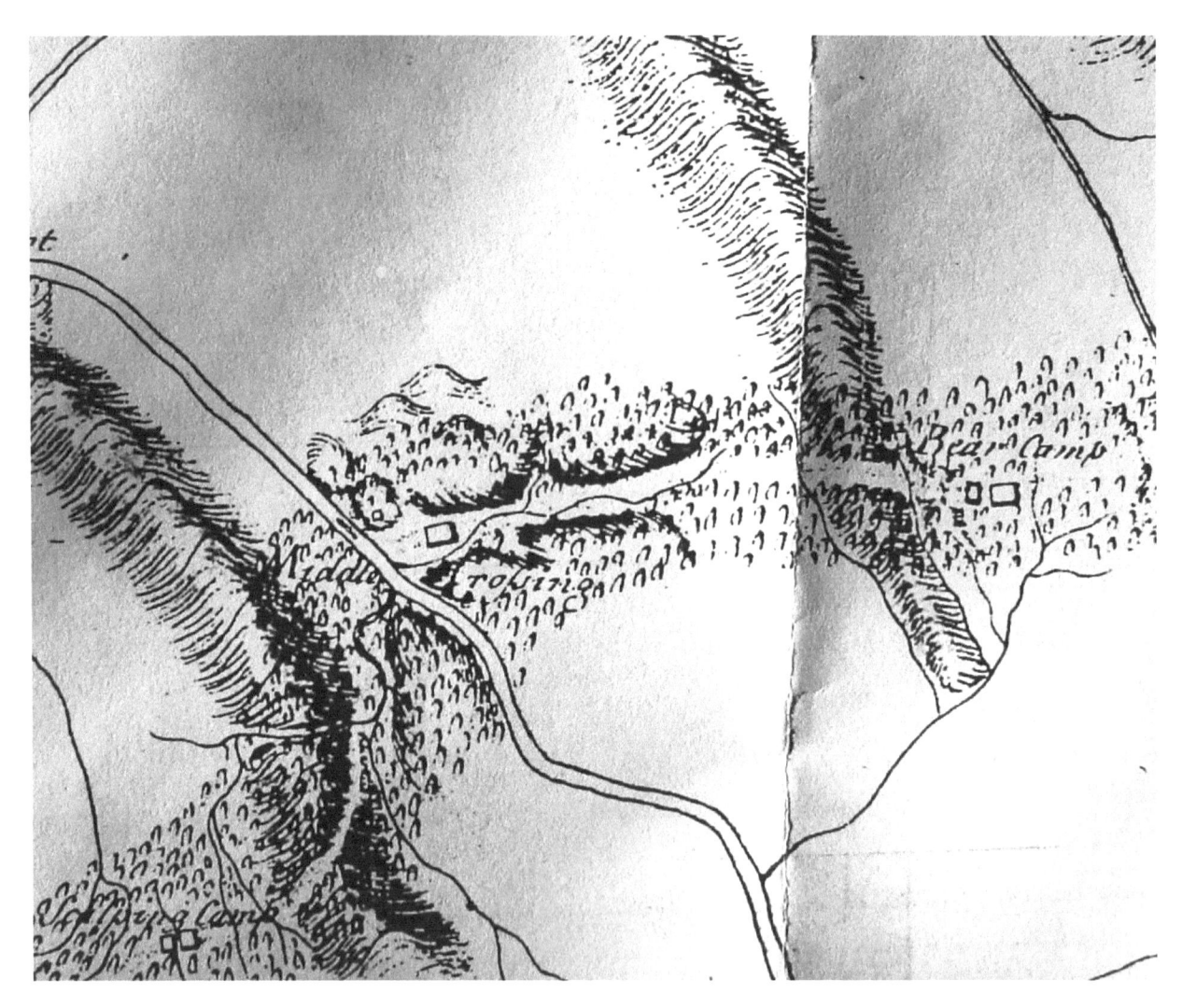

Figure 8 — The *"Gordon map"* shows that, contrary to the 1825 Zer Hagan survey and the 1860 Walker map, Braddock's expedition followed Braddock Run, rather than passing just north of Petersburg (Addison).

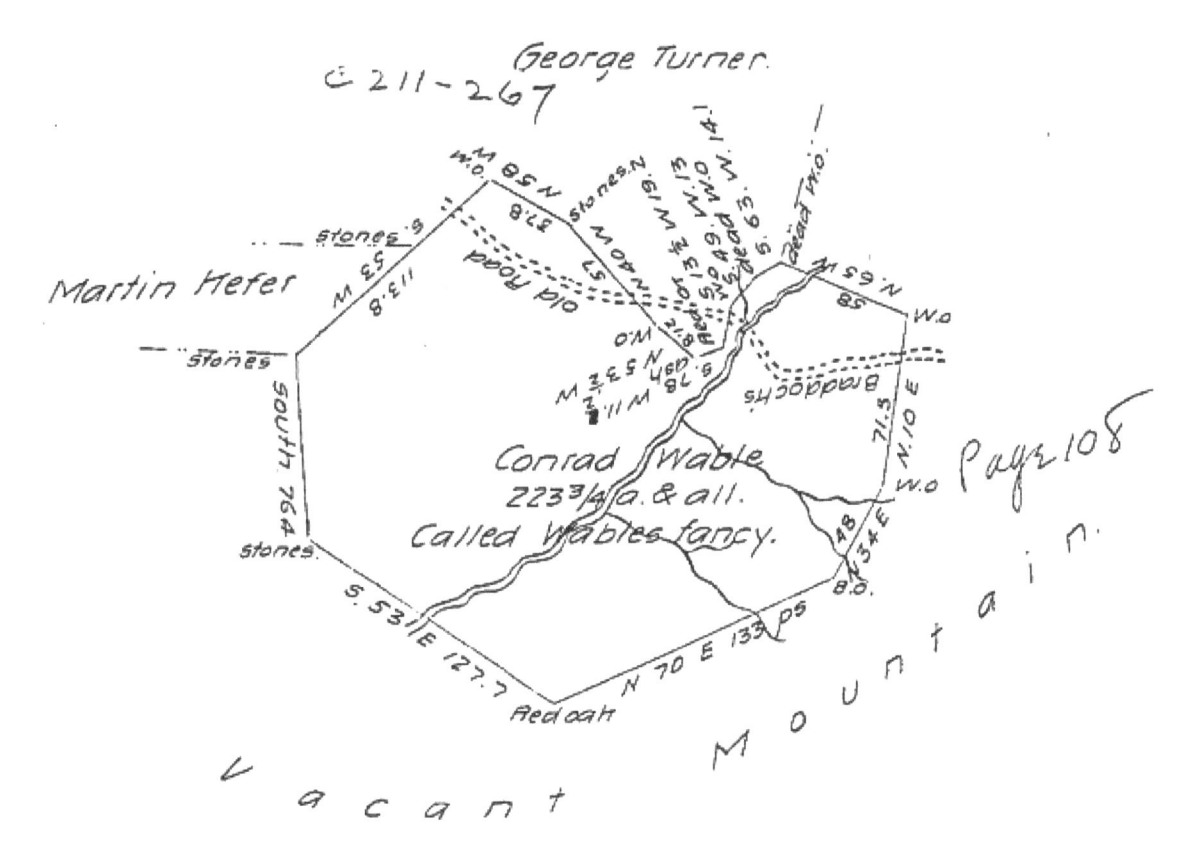

Figure 9 — The 1788 Conrad Wable survey (Book D11, Page 107) is one of the pieces of evidence that helped Robert L. Bantz determine that Braddock's road didn't pass through just north of Petersburg (Addison), and actually followed Braddock Run.

5. Nemacolin's Ohio Company road

John Jacob is the source of all of the multitudinous Nemacolin roadwork stories

John J. Jacob's 1826 book "**A biographical sketch of the life of the late Captain Michael Cresap**" states the following, in reference to Michael Cresap's father Thomas:

It was, perhaps, about this time, or soon after, that...he entered conjointly into an association with two or three gentlemen...and formed what was called "The Ohio Company." This Company made the first English settlement at Pittsburg before Braddock's war; and it was through their means and efforts that the first path was traced through that vast chain of mountains called the Allegheny. Colonel Cresap, as one of that Company, and active agent thereof in this section of the country, employed an honest and friendly Indian to lay out and mark a road from Cumberland to Pittsburg. This Indian's name was Nemacolin; and he did his work so well that General Braddock with his army pursued the same path, which thenceforward took the name of Braddock's road...

Later, in the book, Jacob states, *"The reader has not forgotten, perhaps, that I have already mentioned the name of the Indian Nemacolin, employed by Colonel Cresap to lay out the road to Pittsburg. Now so strong was the affection of this Indian for Colonel Cresap and his family, that he not only spent much of his time with them, but before he finally went away, brought his son George and left him with the family to raise; and it is a fact within my own knowledge that this George lived and died in the family."* These are second-hand accounts by someone who was born several years after the Ohio Company road was opened — but they were written by someone who was very closely associated with the Cresap family.[58] Everything ever written about Nemacolin's roadwork has evolved from these two brief 1826 statements. There was such a road, and it was known by the Indian Nemacolin's name in 1753.[59]

The Ohio Company empowers Thomas Cresap to open a road as far as Turkeyfoot

A May 22, 1751 passage from the *"Orders and Resolutions of the Ohio Company"* includes the following statement:

Resolved that it is necessary to have a Road cleared from the mouth of Wills Creek to the three forks of the Youghogane and that Colo Cresap be empowered to agree with any person or persons willing to undertake the same so that the expense thereof does not exceed twenty-five pounds Virginia currency.

Addressing one argument against the veracity of Jacob's Nemacolin account

One argument I have encountered about the veracity of Jacob's story is that he incorrectly states that the Ohio Company road went to Pittsburgh, when it really only went to the Ohio Company's

---

[58] For more information, see *"An evidence-based look at Nemacolin"* in "**The Casselman Chronicle**" Volume LIV, No 1, 2014.
[59] Maryland Patented Certificate 4993, *"Walnutt Levill"*, patented to John Ross on August 10, 1753, 390 Acres, surveyed June 20, 1753 by Isaac Brooke, MSA S1197-5420.

storehouse on Redstone Creek; i.e. the *"Hangard"*. This argument is easily refuted by the Ohio Company's July 27, 1753 instructions to Christopher Gist, which state:

> *Whereas you have obtained a Commission from the College for Surveying our Lands, You are to provide a measuring wheel at the Companys expense and measure the Road clear'd by the Company from their Store at Wills Creek to the Fork of Mohongaly...*

The reference to *"the Fork of Mohongaly"* is proof that the road went to the site of Pittsburgh — which is where the Ohio Company intended to erect a fort.[60] Their intended site for the fort was near the mouth of Chartiers Creek, a short distance downriver from the forks.

The instruction to Gist uses a place name for the Pittsburgh area that most people are not familiar with today. The following quotes prove that *"the Fork of Mohongaly"* is a reference to the present-day site of Pittsburgh.

Virginia's Lieutenant Governor Robert Dinwiddie referred to the present-day location of Pittsburgh as the *"fork of Monongahela"* in a February 19, 1754 proclamation that states, *"Whereas it is determined that a fort be immediately built on the river Ohio, at the fork of Monongahela, to oppose any further encroachments or hostile attempts of the French and Indians in their interest..."*

The Indians also called the present-day location of Pittsburgh the Fork of the Monongahela. During a June 11, 1752 meeting at Logstown, the Indian Half King said, *"We therefore desire our brethren of Virginia may build a strong house at the Fork of the Mohongalio..."*

In a March 13, 1754 letter to Governor Hamilton, Lieutenant Governor Dinwiddie wrote, *"In January I commissioned William Trent to raise one Hundred men; he had got Seventy and had begun a Fort at the Forks of the Monhongialo."*

In an April 25, 1754 letter to Lieutenant Governor Dinwiddie, written from Wills Creek, Washington wrote, *"Captain Trent's ensign, Mr. Ward, has this day arrived from the Fork of the Monongahela, and brings the disagreeable account, that the fort, on the 17th inst. was surrendered at the summons of Mons. Contrecoeur to a body of French..."*

Ensign Ward's June 30, 1756 deposition makes it clear that Trent started a fort at the *"mouth of the Monongahela"*. Captain Snow's 1754 sketch and colored 1754 map of the Ohio shows a fort at the mouth of the Monongahela, and describes it as *"120 Sq.FT Trent, Drove out by y French, 1754"*.

This is more than enough evidence to establish that the Ohio Company's July 27, 1753 instructions to Christopher Gist describe the Ohio Company road as going to the present-day site of Pittsburgh,

---

[60] The fort was authorized for construction at the July 25 to 27, 1753 Stratford, Westmoreland County, Virginia meeting of the Ohio Company. A record from that meeting includes the statement, *"Resolved that it is absolutely necessary that the Company should immediately erect a Fort for the security and protection of their Settlement on a hill just below Shurtees Creek upon the south east side of the river Ohio ... That Col. Cresap, Capt. Trent, and Mr Gist, be appointed and authorized on behalf of the Company to agree with labourers, Carpenters and other workmen, to build and complete the same as soon as possible..."* The fort was never built.

vindicating John J. Jacob's statement that it did so. We can also reference the 1755 Fry and Jefferson map, which illustrates the existence of such a road prior to Braddock's expedition.[61]

Furthermore, the second petition of the Ohio Company includes the following statement:

> *They then agreed with H. Parker for the carriage of all their goods from the falls of Potomack to their general factory on the River Ohio, and authorized Col. Cresap to have a road opened to those places.*

This definitively states that the Ohio Company intended to have a road opened between the present-day location of Cumberland, Maryland and the Ohio River.

It's not really John J. Jacob's fault that subsequent generations of historians embellished his Nemacolin stories to the point that they are nearly unrecognizable. I find Jacob's Nemacolin account credible because he would have known Thomas Cresap over a period of at least 15 years, and a chapter in his book provides a detailed account of Thomas Cresap's life, suggesting that they had a close personal relationship. It seems reasonable to suspect that Mr. Jacob heard about Nemacolin's work on the Ohio Company road directly from Thomas Cresap.

Mr. Jacob did not claim that Nemacolin opened the Ohio Company road. Instead, he merely claimed that Thomas Cresap employed Nemacolin to "*lay out and mark*" the Ohio Company road that Braddock subsequently followed. This may have involved selecting and marking the most appropriate existing paths to follow.[62]

Washington stated that he and Braddock followed the Ohio Company road

George Washington's August 2, 1758 letter to Colonel Bouquet states, "*…the Ohio Company, in 1753, at a considerable expense, opened the road. In 1754 the troops, whom I had the honor to command, greatly repaired it,*[63] *as far as Gist's plantation;*[64] *and, in 1755, it was widened and completed by General Braddock to within six miles of Fort Duquesne.*" Remember this later.

---

[61] The June 23, 1755 Lewis Evans map also illustrates the road from Fort Cumberland to Fort Duquesne, and provides mileage between various landmarks.

[62] Moravian missionary David Zeisburger's journal entries from October 1767 relate to the Indian footpath known as the Forbidden Path, which whites were forbidden to travel. Even though the journal entries do not relate to a path out of Wills Creek, they may provide insight as to why the Ohio Company needed to hire Nemacolin to lay out and mark an existing, but perhaps lightly used combination of footpaths. One journal entry refers to October 4, 1767, stating, *"It rained on the 4th, yet we continued our journey, finding it difficult to keep to the trail, because often it could not be distinguished. In the evening we had lost it altogether, so that we did not know how to proceed, for Anton and John did not know this region. We, therefore, pitched camp. John walked, the same evening, some distance into the woods, toward the north, to look for the trail. During the night, he returned with the good news that he had found it again."* Zeisberger's October 8, 1767 journal entry states, *"The two Indians with me…had much trouble today in keeping the trail because in places there is for several miles no visible trace of its having been followed by man. Occasionally, we came upon elk tracks (this is a kind of deer that is found in Europe also) which have the appearance of a trail. We were misled by them into a terrible wilderness, so that it was necessary to retrace our steps and stop until John had had an opportunity to go through the woods and find the right trail."* John McMillan's September 1775 journal entry tells a similar story of a losing a faint path in Brothersvalley, north of Fort Cumberland.

[63] For Washington's letters that describe repairing and altering the Ohio Company road, see "**In Search of the Turkey Foot Road**", fourth edition, Dietle & McKenzie.

[64] See Pennsylvania Survey Book C151, page 141 for the location of Christopher Gist's plantation at the present-day site of Mount Braddock, Pennsylvania.

A record describes the improved part of the Ohio Company road

A record from the February 6, 1753 meeting of a committee of the Ohio Company at Marlborough, Stafford County, Virginia indicates that some portion of the Ohio Company road was finished as a wagon road by then.[65] The meeting record, which addresses the inquiry of John Pagan Mercht about the treatment German Protestant settlers would receive, includes this statement:

The Companys Store house at Rock creek where they may land and have their Goods secured is sixty miles from Conococheege a fine road from whence they may go by Water in the Companys Boat to their Store house at Wills Creek about forty miles and from thence the Company have cleared a Waggon Road about sixty miles to one of the head branches of the Ohio[66] *navigable by large flat bottom boats where they proposed to build Storehouse and begin to lay off their Lands.*

Mercer indicates that Washington and Braddock followed the Ohio Company road

George Mercer's December 18, 1769 legal brief in the case of the Ohio Company asserts that the company cleared a road to the present-day location of Pittsburgh. In a section about a February 1753 conflict with William Russell, the brief mentions *"...the road from their storehouse on Will's Creek, to the Ohio (and which they had been at the expense of clearing)..."* Speaking from his own knowledge, George Mercer asserted that the Ohio Company traced out and completed the road to the Ohio River that Washington used in 1754 and Braddock used in 1755, stating, *"Your memorialist presumes to inform your majesty, that the first actual survey of that country, was made*

---

[65] George Washington's May 9, 1754 letter to Dinwiddie from the Little Meadows is the earliest written proof I have seen of anyone actually using a wagon on the Ohio Company road. It includes the statement, *"I acquainted you by Mr. Ward with the determination, which we prosecuted four days after his departure, as soon as wagons arrived to carry our provisions."* Prior to that, while traveling east from Gist's plantation on January 6, 1754, Washington encountered a packhorse train with 17 horses *"loaded with materials and stores for a fort at the fork of the Ohio."* This seems to have been an Ohio Company activity, because Washington's subsequent March 31, 1754 marching orders from Dinwiddie mention *"the Fort w'ch I expect is there already begun by the Ohio Comp'a."* Gist may have taken a wagon to his plantation before Washington's May 9, 1754 letter. Gist's application for compensation, which was recorded in the House of Burgesses on October 30, 1754, states, *"His Majesty's forces, under the command of Colonel Washington, encamped at the petitioner's plantation, and his Horses and Carriage being employed in his Majesty's services, he was thereby prevented from removing the greatest part of his effects..."* It isn't clear whether Gist's wagon accompanied Washington's expedition from Wills Creek, or preceded it.

[66] The Ohio Company sometimes exaggerated their accomplishments, and this seems to be one such exaggeration. It is doubtful that their wagon road went as far as stated, based on three written statements by Washington, as he attempted to open a wagon road to Redstone. Washington's journal for May 16, 1754 indicates there was no wagon road to Redstone at the time, stating, *"Met two traders, who told us they fled for fear of the French as parties of them were often seen toward Mr. Gist's. These traders are of opinion, as well as many others, that it is not possible to clear a road for loaded wagons to go from hence to Red-Stone-Creek."* In a May 18, 1754 letter to Dinwiddie, written from the Great Crossings, Washington wrote, *"These Indians, and all the traders that I have been able to get any information from, of late, agree, that it is almost impracticable to open a road that a wagon can pass from this to Red-stone Creek."* Washington's June 27, 1754 journal entry states, *"June 27. Detached Captain Lewis, Lieutenant Waggoner and Ensign Mercer, two Sergeants, two Corporals, one drummer and sixty men, in order to endeavor to clear a road to the mouth of RedStone Creek, on Monongahela."* For another example of exaggeration, the second petition of the Ohio Company states that they *"laid out and opened a wagon road thirty feet wide from their Store house at Wills Creek, to the three branches on Ganyangaine River, computed to be near Eighty Miles"*. If their wagon road was really thirty feet wide, then surely the forces of Washington and Braddock would have had little need to improve the road to handle military traffic. Orme's journal confirms that Braddock's forces did have to improve the Ohio Company road, stating, *"There was also an advanced party of three hundred men to precede the line to cut and make the roads..."*

at the company's expense, and that the road from Will's Creek to the Ohio, the route of your majesty's troops in 1754, and 1755, was not only traced out, but compleated entirely at the company's charge..."

The road the Ohio company completed to the Ohio River was not capable of handling military traffic, but Washington did follow and improve the road in 1754, and Braddock did follow and further improve the road in 1755. Braddock did deviate from the Ohio Company road on at least one occasion, crossing and re-crossing the Monongahela River to avoid a dangerous defile.

A survey references the location of Nemacolin's Ohio Company road

The previously quoted statements suggest that one might begin looking for Braddock's route in the vicinity of Frostburg by trying to identify the route of the Ohio Company road, which was contemporaneously referred to as Nemacolin's road. Fortuitously, the June 23, 1753 Walnutt Levill survey does just that, stating:

Laid out for and in the name of him the said Ross all that Tract Called Walnutt Levill Beginning at a Bounded black oak standing on the Head of a Branch of Nill Creek[67] about a mile from Nehemiah Collins road and running thence West three hundred and eight p North ten Degrees West three hundred and twenty Perches South fifty Degrees East two hundred and eighty perches South Fifty Degrees East one hundred perches. Then by a straight line to the Beginning Tree Containing and now Laid out for three hundred and Ninety acres of Land to be held of Conegocheige Mannor Surveyd this twentieth Day of June – 1753

"*Nehemiah Collins*" is an Anglicization of the name Nemacolin. Two other contemporaneous variations of Nemacolin's name that have survived in historical transcripts are "*Neal McCollen*" and "*Nimach Collins*".[68]

Figure 10 shows the image from the Walnutt Levill survey, rotated so that north is at the top. The starting point at the "*Bounded black oak standing on the Head of a Branch of Nill Creek about a mile from Nehemiah Collins road*" is identified with an icon of a tree. Veatch's map[69] of Francis Deakins' survey of lots westward of Fort Cumberland (Figure 11) shows the location of Walnutt Levill relative to the Mountain tract, and other tracts in the vicinity of Frostburg.

The northernmost point of the Walnutt Levill survey is shown on the 1953 map[70] of Frostburg that is included as Figure 12. This acute corner is located at approximately latitude 39.649257°,

---

[67] This is a reference to a tributary of Preston Run, one of the headwaters of Braddock Run, which is a tributary of Wills Creek.

[68] For more information, see *"An evidence-based look at Nemacolin"* in **"The Casselman Chronicle"** Volume LIV, No 1, 2014. I didn't come to the realization that *"Nehemiah Collins"* was an Anglicization of the name Nemacolin until Cumberland Road Historian Steve Colby was near death, and unable to discuss the subject. Several years prior to his death, however, Steve and I searched diligently for a person named Nehemiah Collins in early western Maryland, and found nothing.

[69] Although not germane to this study, the 1774 *"Policy"* survey (MSA S1208 762) on Veatch's map can be used to identify the location of Braddock's road west of Frostburg, because the 1796 survey *"Resurvey on Policy"* (MSA S1211 747) states, *"....at the original beginning, it being a bounded chesnut standing about 25 feet south of Braddocks old road and about 2 miles west of Georges Creek...."* (These surveys were found by Julia Jackson.)

[70] This map was provided by John Devault.

longitude -78.931348°. The second line of the survey is described as, *"North ten Degrees West three hundred and twenty Perches"*. The cosine of 10° times 320 perches equals 315.138 perches, or 0.977 miles. The sine of 10° times 320 perches equals 55.567 perches, or 0.172 miles. The first line of the survey is described as, *"West three hundred and eight p"*, which equals 0.955 miles. The sum of 0.172 miles and 0.955 miles equals 1.127 miles. Taken together, this means that the starting point of the Walnutt Levill survey is 0.977 miles (5,159 feet) south of its northernmost tip, and 1.127 miles east. This puts the starting point at approximately latitude 39.635203°, longitude -78.909831°, in Hoffman Hollow near a distinctive crook in Hoffman Hollow Road SW.

The Walnutt Levill survey states that the starting point *is "about a mile from Nehemiah Collins road"*. Unfortunately, the surveyor did not mention a compass direction in connection with this one mile distance. As an exercise in logic, one can imagine a circle with a one-mile radius that is centered on the starting point of the survey. According to the survey, at least one portion of Nemacolin's road would have been located somewhere approximately on this circle. Extending the logic further, no part of Nemacolin's road would have been located well-inside the circle, and all of the road that wasn't located approximately on the circle would have been located somewhere outside of the circle. This line of reasoning rules out Hoffman Hollow as the location of Nemacolin's road, especially considering that the starting point of the survey is located right in Hoffman Hollow. This also rules out all of Lacock's postulated route of Braddock's road between Hoffman Hollow and Grahamtown as being any part of Nemacolin's road. The valley of Porter Run is the only viable alternative to Hoffman Hollow for the Ohio Company road, so it seems safe to conclude that the Ohio Company road followed the valley of Porter Run. The difficulties that would have been encountered in opening a new wagon road through Hoffman Hollow seem like a compelling[71] reason for Braddock's engineers to follow the Ohio Company road along Porter Run in 1755.

One can look at the terrain shown in Figure 1 to find interesting spots to check the *"about a mile"* statement against. The starting point of Walnutt Levill is 1.20 miles west-southwest of where the Old National Road crosses Preston Run at Clarysville. We might construe this to be *"about a mile"*, but a surveyor trying to identify the location of the starting point of a survey in a howling wilderness might not. The valley of Porter Run between Clarysville and the village of Eckhart Mines is well outside of the circle, and is the only viable terrain candidate outside of the circle for the Ohio Company road to follow west. The valley of Porter Run is harmonious with the route of Braddock's road that is schematically illustrated on the maps of Gist, Gordon, and Orme, which are included herein and described below. The route illustrated on those maps is not harmonious with the routes espoused by Atkinson, Middleton, and Lacock.

One mile north of the starting point is another likely terrain location, at approximately latitude 39.649729°, longitude -78.909993°. This is about 180 feet southeast of where the Old National Pike SW comes out on the New Georges Creek Road SW (Route 36) at the eastern edge of present-day Frostburg. This set of GPS coordinates is west of and at the same latitude as the village of Eckhart Mines. The section of the Old National Road between Clarysville and the aforementioned

---

[71] This sentence is paraphrased from an observation made by Dave Williams.

GPS coordinates is harmonious with the route that is schematically illustrated on the maps of Gist, Gordon, and Orme — but this isn't hard evidence that the Old National Road followed the Ohio Company Road closely, and isn't proof that the Ohio Company road actually passed through the aforementioned coordinates.

There is a surviving section of an old sunken road that is located between the aforementioned coordinates and either projected site of the second camp. Robert L. Bantz states that it is located between the cemetery and Route 36, to the north of the present-day golf course. He did not indicate the bearing or precise location of the sunken road, and even if its bearing fits well with the route theory presented herein, it could conceivably just be part of the U-shaped trail that is illustrated in that general area on Figure 1. Nevertheless, we could simply declare it to be Braddock's road, and have just as much proof as Lacock presented for the route from Hoffman Hollow to Grahamtown – which is to say precisely none.

Another interesting point on the circle is approximately where Walnut Street enters the Allegany Cemetery. This is but a short distance due east of where the traditional route of Braddock's road through Frostburg fades out a little eastward of Grant Street on the 1953 map of Figure 12. It is not difficult to imagine a route on an easy grade that is located on or outside of the circle that connects this location with the valley of Porter Run in the vicinity of the village of Eckhart Mines. I hope the readers of this book will research early properties on and north of the circle for possible references to Braddock's road.[72]

Addressing an argument against the Walnutt Levill survey

A well-respected historian who disagrees with the theory presented in this book makes the argument that the Walnutt Levill reference to Nemacolin's road could be a reference to an antecedent to Route 36 between Frostburg and Lonaconing, since tradition has Nemacolin's son George living at Lonaconing,[73] and Nemacolin may have traveled that antecedent to visit George. Personally, I view the Walnutt Levill reference as confirming John Jacob's statement that Nemacolin was hired to *"lay out and mark"* the Ohio Company road. I also view the Walnutt Levill reference as validating Judge James Veech's use of the term *"Nemacolin's road"* in his 1857 book "**Mason And Dixons Line: A History**". Furthermore, I view Washington's map of his journey to the French forts with Christopher Gist, and the January 1, 1755 illustration of the Ohio Company road on the 1755 Fry and Jefferson map (both described later in this book) as

---

[72] There happens to be an interesting but yet-unidentified linear feature that is visible on LIDAR and has the appearance of a sunken road. It is located on the hillside just east of Route 36 at approximately latitude 39.648767°, longitude -78.908633°. There are also interesting but yet-unidentified trail-like linear features on the south side of the creek in the village of Eckhart Mines, at approximately latitude 39.651554°, longitude -78.898886°. There also seems to be faint evidence of a filled in sunken road across the Allegany Cemetery, at the right location to connect the traditional route of Braddock's road through Frostburg to the village of Eckhart Mines. These features warrant on-the-ground investigation, but until then, can't be counted as anything.

[73] The earliest written account of the Georges Creek naming tradition that I have found is Horatio N. Parker's *"Historical Sketch of the Potomac Basin"* in the 1907 book "**House Documents**" from the 59th Congress. The source and accuracy of Parker's naming tradition is unknown. The article states, *"Georges Creek took its name from an Indian, George, who had his hunting lodge on the present site of Lonaconing. He was a favorite of, and lived with Col. Thomas Cresap, of Oldtown, who had employed his father, Nemacolin, to mark out the road from Cumberland to Brownsville, on the Monongahela."*

reasonable evidence that Nemacolin's Ohio Company road passed through the site of present-day Frostburg on a generally east-west heading.

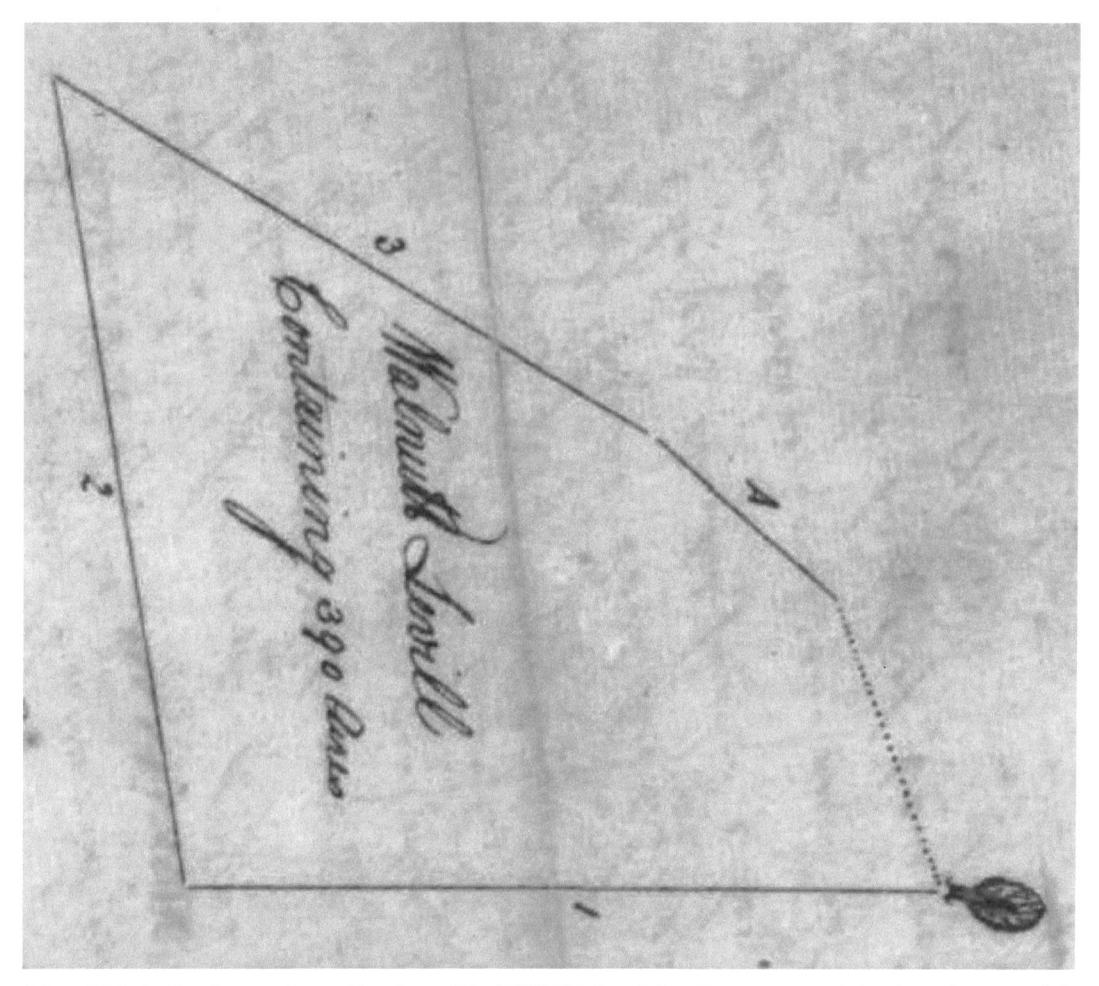

Figure 10 — This is the image from the June 23, 1753 Walnutt Levill survey, rotated so that north is at the top of the page. The starting point, identified with the icon of a tree, is located in Hoffman Hollow. Nemacolin's Ohio Company road was about a mile from this starting point.

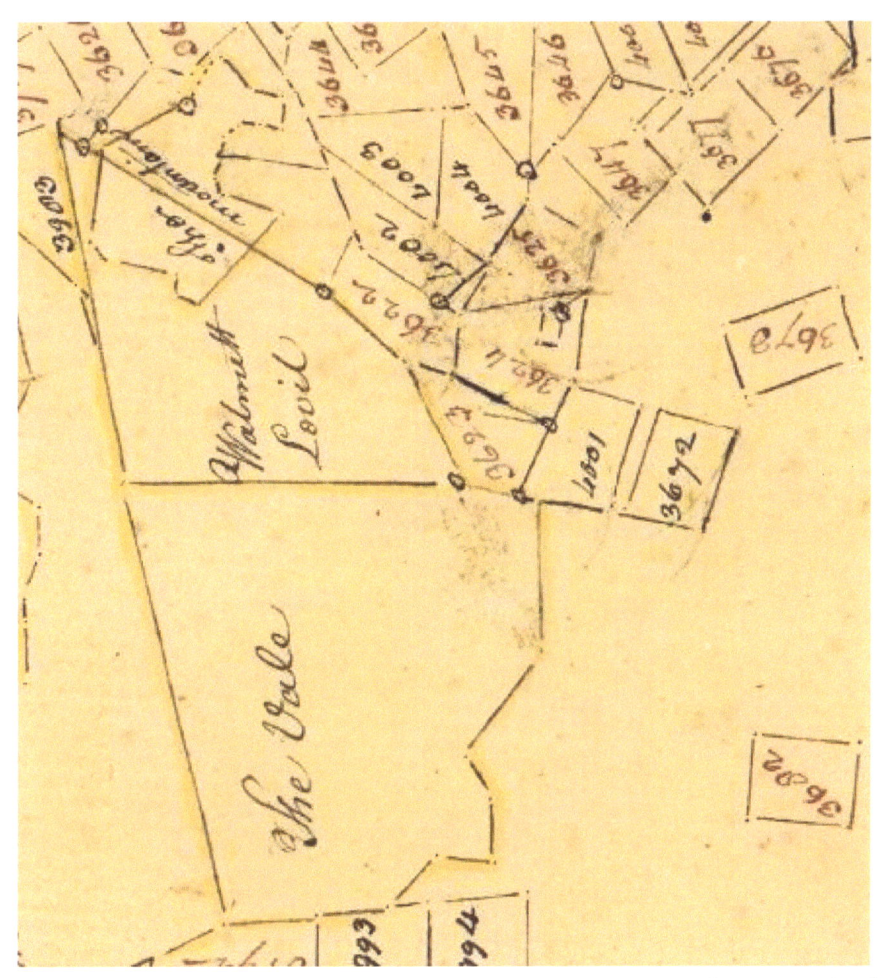

Figure 11 — This is from Veatch's map of Francis Deakins' surveys west of Fort Cumberland (Library of Congress Call No. G3843.G3G46 1787 .V4). It shows the relative locations of the Walnutt Levill and Mountain surveys. The 1775 survey for *"The Vale"* mentions, *"Beginning at the end of the first line of a Tract of Land Called Walnut Level"*, but makes no mention of a road.

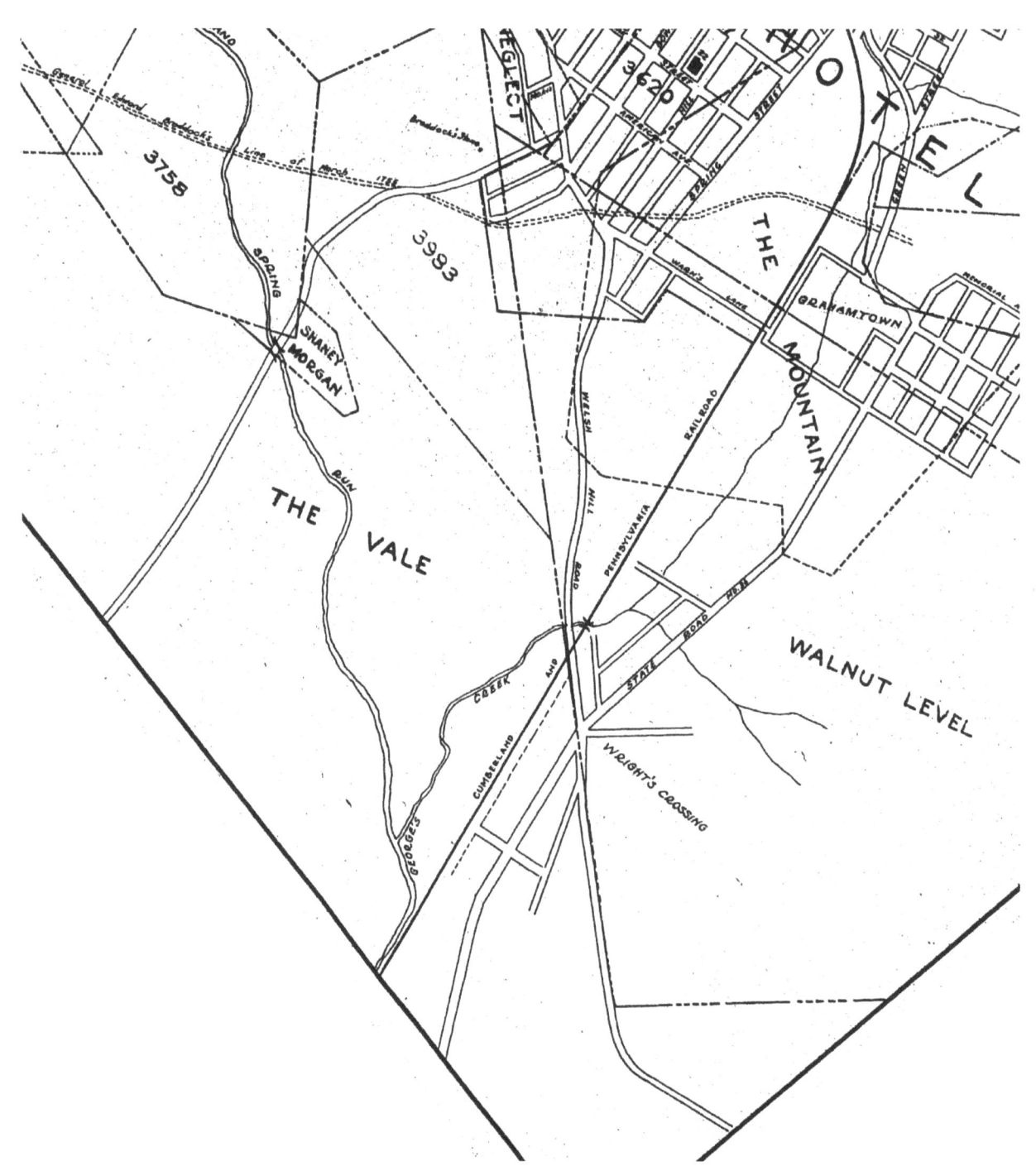

Figure 12 — This is from a 1953 map of Frostburg, Maryland. It shows some of the original surveys of the area, and shows the traditional route of Braddock's road through Frostburg. Several fragments of this route still survive.

6. Gist was involved with opening the Ohio Company road

The Ohio Company records show Gist's involvement in the company road

Contemporaneous evidence shows that Christopher Gist was deeply involved in opening the Ohio Company road that Braddock later followed. The Ohio Company's July 16, 1751 instructions to Christopher Gist were:

> *After You have returned from Williamsburg and have executed the Commission of the President & Council, if they shall think proper to give You One, otherwise as soon as You can conveniently You are to apply to Col. Cresap for such of the Company's Horses, as You shall want for the Use of yourself and such other Person or Persons You shall think necessary to carry with You; and You are to look out & observe the nearest & most convenient Road You can find from the Company's Store at Wills's Creek to a Landing at Mohongeyela...*

Christopher Gist began his journey of discovery for the Ohio Company on November 4, 1751, and wrote the following journal entry that describes following Braddock Run:

> *1751.—Pursuant to my Instructions hereunto annexed from the Committee of the Ohio Company bearing Date 16th July 1751*
>
> *Monday Novr 4.—Set out from the Company's Store House in Frederick County Virginia opposite the Mouth of Wills's Creek and crossing Potomack River went W 4 M to a Gap in the Allegany Mountains upon the S W Fork of the said Creek – This Gap is the nearest to Potomack River of any in the Allegany Mountains, and is accounted one of the best, tho the Mountain is very high, The Ascent is no where very steep but rises gradually near 6 M, it is now very full of old Trees & Stones, but with some Pains might be made a good Waggon Road; this Gap is directly in the Way to Mohongaly, & several Miles nearer than that the Traders commonly pass thro, and a much better Way.*[74]

The Ohio Company's April 28, 1752 instructions to Christopher Gist state:

> *If Col Cresap has not agreed with any person to clear a Road for the Company, you are with the advice and assistance of Col. Cresap to agree with the proper Indians, who are best acquainted with the ways, immediately to cut a road from Wills Creek to the Fork of Mohongaly at the cheapest Rate you can for Goods, and this you may mention publicly to the Indians at the Loggs Town or not as you see occasion.*

In this quote, the *"Fork of Mohongaly"* is the present-day site of Pittsburgh, as explained elsewhere herein.

---

[74] For detailed analysis of this journal entry, see "**In Search of the Turkey Foot Road**", fourth edition, Dietle & McKenzie.

Indians from the Ohio valley help to open a road to a tributary of the Ohio

A December 10, 1752 letter from Lieutenant Governor Dinwiddie to the Board of Trade indicates that part of the Ohio Company road was opened with the help of Indians from the Ohio River drainage basin, stating:

> *...the Indians on the Ohio have opened a road from a river that runs into the Ohio to the head of Potomac river, in this Dominion, with a land-carriage only of eighty miles, which will be of great use to our settlers and traders, as also for the conveying of our cannon to proper places on the above river.*

This quote may be a reference to a road to the mouth of Redstone Creek, near where Nemacolin was living in December, 1752.[75] Bear in mind that this December 10, 1752 letter was written long before the Ohio Company instructed Christopher Gist to *measure the Road clear'd by the Company from their Store at Wills Creek to the Fork of Mohongaly..."* (now Pittsburgh) on July 27, 1753. Based on the correspondence and maps presented herein, it appears that the Ohio Company initially opened a road to the Monongahela River, and then opened a branch road to the mouth of the Monongahela River. Bear in mind that the use of the word *"road"* back then did not always imply a wagon road. Footpaths were sometimes referred to as roads, and over time, such footpaths were often upgraded to more easily handle packhorse traffic.

The Ohio Company paid Christopher Gist for opening their road

According to Lois Mulkearn's 1954 book "**George Mercer Papers: Relating to the Ohio Company of Virginia**" and Alfred Proctor James' 1959 book "**The Ohio Company: Its Inner History**", the minutes from the July 1753 Ohio Company meeting contain an order that the company treasurer pay 44 pounds, 16 shillings to Christopher Gist for having made a road between Wills Creek and *"Mohongaly"*. The quotes of the minutes in the two books are slightly different. Mulkearn's quote says that the 44-pound, 16-shilling payment is compensation for 56 pounds in Maryland currency that Gist expended to have the road made. This payment to Christopher Gist is reasonable evidence that Christopher Gist participated in opening the Ohio Company road.

---

[75] Christopher Gist's December 7, 1752 journal entry describes visiting an Indian camp near what is now known as Dunlap Creek, and having a long discussion with Nemacolin. To get from Nemacolin's camp to a rock shelter that Gist describes in detail in his December 9, 1752 journal entry, Gist *"Set out S 45 1 M, W 6 M to the River Mohongaly"*. Endnote 197 in Mulkearn's 1954 book "**George Mercer Papers: Relating to the Ohio Company of Virginia**" reports that there is a rock shelter with a smooth floor along Wallace Run, ¼ mile from its mouth. Wallace Run enters the Monongahela River at latitude 39.92649°, longitude -79.925537°. Mulkearn interprets Gist's journal as putting Nemacolin's camp somewhere along Dunlaps Creek, rather than at its mouth. This means that Mulkearn interprets Gist's *"S 45 1 M"* as traveling southwest one mile. Burd's September 22, 1759 journal entry references *"Nemocollin's Creek"*, and his September 30, 1759 letter references *"Nemoraling's Creek, on the Monongahela, about one mile above the mouth or Redstone Creek"*.

An assessment for clearing the road and building the fort at Chartiers Creek

The following quote[76] is from a November 2, 1753 meeting of the Ohio Company:

Agreed and Ordered that each member of the Company pay to Mr. George Mason their Treasurer, the sum of twenty pounds current money for building and finishing the Fort at Shurtees Creek, Grubing and clearing the road from the Company's store at Wills Creek to the Mohongaly, which are to be finished with the utmost dispatch and for such other purposes as shall be directed by the Company.

---

[76] **"Christopher Gist's Journals…"**, Darlington, 1893.

7. Washington followed the Ohio Company road in 1753

Washington is commissioned to deliver a message to the French forts

On October 30, 1753, Dinwiddie wrote[77] instructions for George Washington that state:

Whereas I have received information of a body of French forces being assembled in a hostile manner on the river Ohio, intending by force of arms to erect certain forts on the said river within this territory, and contrary to the dignity and peace of our sovereign the King of Great Britain;

These are, therefore, to require and direct you, the said George Washington, forthwith to repair to Logstown on the said river Ohio; and, having there informed yourself where the said French forces have posted themselves, thereupon to proceed to such place; and, being there arrived, to present your credentials, together with my letter to the chief commanding officer, and in the name of his Britannic Majesty to demand an answer thereto.

On your arrival at Logstown you are to address yourself to the Half-King, to Monacatoocha, and other the sachems of the Six Nations, acquainting them with your orders to visit and deliver my letter to the French commanding officer, and desiring the said chiefs to appoint you a sufficient number of their warriors to be your safeguard, as near the French as you may desire, and to wait your further direction.

You are diligently to inquire into the numbers and force of the French on the Ohio, and the adjacent country; how they are likely to be assisted from Canada; and what are the difficulties and conveniences of that communication, and the time required for it.

You are to take care to be truly informed what forts the French have erected, and where; how they are garrisoned, and appointed, and what is their distance from each other, and from Logstown; and from the best intelligence you can procure, you are to learn what gave occasion to this expedition of the French; how they are likely to be supported, and what their pretensions are.

When the French commandant has given you the required and necessary despatches, you are to desire of him a proper guard to protect you as far on your return, as you may judge for your safety, against any straggling Indians or hunters, that may be ignorant of your character, and molest you.

Wishing you good success in your negotiation, and a safe and speedy return, I am, &c.

Robert Dinwiddie.

Williamsburg, 30 October, 1753.

---

[77] For other documents concerning Washington's assignment, including his commission, written pass, the letter he delivered, and the French reply, see "**Fort Cumberland: The missing years**", Dietle, 2016.

George Washington travels with Gist on the Ohio Company road

In 1753, Christopher Gist accompanied Washington on Washington's trip from Wills Creek to *"deliver a letter to the commandant of the French forces on the Ohio"*. Gist's journal from the trip includes the statement:

> *Wednesday 14 November, 1753. — Then Major George Washington came to my house at Will's Creek, and delivered me a letter from the council in Virginia, requesting me to attend him up to the commandant of the French fort on the Ohio River.*

Washington's November 15, 1753 journal entry shows that he hired Christopher Gist to guide him on the journey. The journal entry includes the following statement:

> *... we pursued the new Road to Wills Creek, where we arrived on the 14th of November.*

> *Here I engaged Mr. Gist to pilot us out, and also hired four others as Servitors, Barnaby Currin and John Mac-Quire, Indian Traders, Henry Steward, and William Jenkins; and in company with those persons, left the Inhabitants the Day following.*

Washington's map of his journey to the French forts

The Library of Congress facsimile copy of a schematic map (Figure 13) that accompanied George Washington's 1754 "**Journal to the Ohio**" shows that he followed Braddock Run, and crossed the distinctive headwaters of Georges Creek in the vicinity of present-day Frostburg. Gist's November 15, 1753 journal entry from the trip states, *"Thursday 15. — We set out, and at night encamped at George's Creek, about eight miles..."*[78]

Washington's map indicates that he and Gist followed the road that Gist opened for the Ohio Company,[79] and indicates that road passed through the location of Frostburg. As quoted above, Mercer wrote that Braddock followed the Ohio Company road. As also quoted above, in 1758, Washington wrote that his troops repaired the Ohio Company road in 1754, and Braddock widened it in 1755. Having participated in Braddock's expedition, Washington's statement carries a great deal of weight. The evidence that Washington's 1754 expedition and Braddock's 1755 expedition followed the Ohio Company road cannot, however, be interpreted as meaning that those expeditions literally followed the exact route of the Ohio Company road every step of the way.

---

[78] This shows that Georges Creek was already known by its present name in 1753.

[79] Washington's map shows a distinctive turn at Gist's plantation that Braddock's subsequent road followed. This turn is visible on a 1939 aerial photo. Shippen's 1759 map also depicts the northward turn of Braddock's road just west of Gist's. This helps to substantiate that Braddock, at least in general, followed the Ohio Company road. Unlike Braddock's route, however, Washington's route stayed on the east side of the Monongahela River.

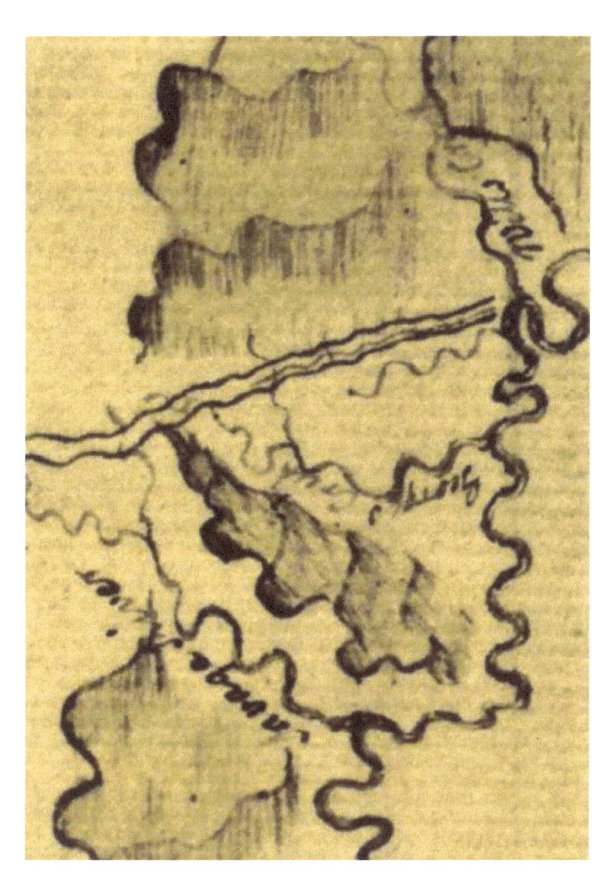

Figure 13 — This image is from a facsimile of a map George Washington created to document his 1753 journey (Library of Congress Call No. G3820 1754 .W3 1927 TIL). It shows the Ohio Company road following what would become known as Braddock Run, and crossing the head forks of Georges Creek. Another copy of the map, not included here, was drawn from the original at the British Museum by James A. Burt in 1882. It omits Braddock Run, but shows the Ohio Company road crossing the head forks of Georges Creek.

8. Washington improved the Ohio Company road in 1754

Washington's receives his marching orders

Washington's March 31, 1754 orders[80] from Lieutenant Governor Dinwiddie commanded him as follows:

Instruct's to be observd by Maj'r Geo. Washington, on the Expedit'n to the Ohio.

MAJ'R GEO. WASHINGTON: You are forthwith to repair to the Co'ty of Frederick and there to take under Y'r Com'd 50 Men of the Militia who will be deliver'd to You by the Comd'r of the s'd Co'ty pursuant to my Orders. You are to send Y'r Lieut, at the same Time to the Co'ty of Augusta, to receive 50 Men from the Comd'r of that Co'ty as I have order'd, and with them he is to join You at Alexandria, to which Place You are to proceed as soon as You have rec'd the Men in Frederick. Having rec'd the Detachm't, You are to train and discipline them in the best Manner You can, and for all Necessaries You are to apply Y'rself to Mr. Jno. Carlisle at Alex'a who has my Orders to supply You. Having all Things in readiness You are to use all Expedition in proceeding to the Fork of Ohio with the Men under Com'd and there you are to finish and compleat in the best Manner and as soon as You possibly can, the Fort w'ch I expect is there already begun by the Ohio Comp'a. You are to act on the Defensive, but in Case any Attempts are made to obstruct the Works or interrupt our Settlem'ts by any Persons whatsoever You are to restrain all such Offenders, and in Case of resistance to make Prisoners of or kill and destroy them. For the rest You are to conduct Y'rself as the Circumst's of the Service shall require and to act as You shall find best for the Furtherance of His M'y's Service and the Good of His Dom'n. Wishing You Health and Success I bid you Farewell.

Washington's writings concerning 1754 work on the Ohio Company road

Less than a week after Ward's April 17, 1754 ejection from the beginnings of a fort at the mouth of the Monongahela River, and immediately upon hearing the news, George Washington convened a council of war, on April 23, 1754. Washington's journal records the council of war as follows:

It was thought a thing impracticable to march towards the Fort without sufficient strength; however, being strongly invited by the Indians, and particularly by the speeches of the Half-King, the president put the question to vote whether we should not advance, as far as Red-Stone Creek on Monongahela about thirty-seven miles on this side of the fort, and there to erect a fortification, clearing a road broad enough to pass with all our artillery and our baggage, and there to wait for fresh Orders.

The proposition aforesaid was adopted for the following reasons;

---

[80] The orders are printed in Toner's 1893 book "**Journal of Colonel George Washington: commanding a detachment of Virginia Troops**". Toner provides no date. Washington's 1754 journal does provide the date, stating, "On the 31st of March I received from his honor a Lieutenant Colonel's commission, of the Virginia regiment, whereof Joshua Fry, Esq., was Colonel, dated the 15th, with orders to take the troops which were at that time at Alexandria, under my command, and to march with them towards the Ohio, there to help Captain Trent to build forts, and to defend the possessions of his Majesty against the attempts and hostilities of the French."

1st. That the mouth of Red-Stone is the first convenient place on the River Monongahela.

2nd. The stores are already built at that place for the provisions of the Company, wherein our Ammunition may be laid up, our great guns may be also sent by water whenever we shall think it convenient to attack the Fort.

In an April 25, 1754 letter George Washington wrote to Lieutenant Governor Dinwiddie from Wills Creek, concerning the work on the Ohio Company road that he planned to have his troops perform, he stated that his objective was *"...to make the road sufficiently good for the heaviest artillery to pass..."*

In theory, Washington could have switched the route from Porter Run to Hoffman Hollow. The problem with this idea, though, is there wasn't much time for such a thing. In a May 9, 1754 letter to Lieutenant Governor Dinwiddie, sent from Little Meadows, Washington states:

...I detached a party of sixty men to make and mend the road, which party since the 25th of April, and the main body since the 1st instant, have been laboriously employed, and have got no farther than these Meadows, about twenty miles from the New Store. We have been two days making a bridge across the river, and have not done yet.

The great difficulty and labor, that it requires to mend and alter the road, prevent our marching above two, three, or four miles a day; and I fear, though no diligence shall be spared, that we shall be detained some considerable time before it can be made good for the carriage of the artillery with Colonel Fry.

In a May 18, 1754 letter to Dinwiddie, written from the Great Crossings, Washington states:

As the road to this place is made as good as it can be, having spent much time and great labor upon it, I believe wagons may travel now with 1500 or 1800 weight on them, by doubling teams at one or two pinches only.

There were only 60 men in Washington's road crew, they were intending to ultimately push a wagon road through to Redstone (Brownsville), and they had mended the road as far as the Great Crossings after more than three weeks of hard labor. One has to wonder if they really had enough manpower and time, and a reasonable motive, to perform a major route alteration to what the Ohio Company described as being a *"Waggon Road"* to potential customers on February 6, 1753. As quoted above, in 1758 Washington wrote that his 1754 road work involved repairing the road that the Ohio Company opened *"at a considerable expense"* in 1753. Just as it seems like Braddock had a compelling reason to follow Washington's road in 1755, it seems like Washington had a compelling reason to follow the Ohio Company road as far as he could in 1754 — it would have been much easier and quicker, compared to opening a new road. As quoted previously, on August 2, 1758, Washington explicitly stated that he and Braddock did follow the Ohio Company road.

The 1755 Fry and Jefferson map shows the Ohio Company road

Although conspicuously marked 1751, the Fry and Jefferson map (Figure 14) was printed in in London in 1755. It illustrates a wagon road going as far as Fort Necessity. Past Fort Necessity, the map only shows a path to Fort Duquesne, and unlike Braddock's road, the path stays on the east side of the Monongahela River. Fort Duquesne is identified as the *"Fort taken 1754 called by the French F. du Quesne"*. The map includes a table that includes the distances from Williamsburg, Fredricksburg, and Alexandria to Fort Necessity, and states, *"These Distances with the Course of the Roads on the Map I carefully collected on the Spot and enterd them in my Journal from whence they are now inserted. J. Dalrymple — London Jany ye 1st 1755."* This statement proves that the map illustrates the Ohio Company wagon road — with the understanding that Dalrymple may have measured the distances during or after the period George Washington repaired the road as far as the Great Meadows between April 25, 1754 and May 18, 1754.

The 1755 Fry and Jefferson map illustrates the road westward from Fort Cumberland as passing through the headwaters of Georges Creek, although the creek is named *"Lonaconin Creek"* on that map.[81] This is harmonious with Washington's depiction of the Ohio Company road passing through the headwaters of Georges Creek on his map (Figure 13) of his 1753 journey to the French forts. When viewed in the context of the early maps of Braddock's road, these maps suggest that Braddock's expedition followed the route of Nemacolin's Ohio Company road in the vicinity of Frostburg. This weighs against the Hoffman Hollow route, because as proven herein by the Walnutt Levill survey, the Ohio Company road did not follow Hoffman Hollow.

A 1754 record describes the Ohio Company wagon road

Volume II of the 1853 edition of the "**Pennsylvania Archives**" states that there was a 52-mile-long wagon road from Wills Creek to the Great Meadows in 1754. Although the month of the 1754 route description is not given, it is presented between records from April 2, 1754 and June 3, 1754. Based on this, the route description may have been prepared sometime around the April 25, 1754 to May 18, 1754 period when Washington was repairing that part of the Ohio Company road. The description reads:

FROM MOUTH OF WILLS CR. ON POTOMAC.
New Store at the Mouth of Wills Creek on Potommick, to Cresaps, 15 miles.
From Wills Creek to ye Great Meadows, a Waggon Road, 52
From ye Great Meadows to Gists,   .   .   10
To the Crossin of Ohiogany,   .   .   .   6
To the Mouth of Mehongielo,   .   .   .   40
                                                          ———
                                                          108

From Rags town to ye Big Meadows,   .   .   70
Indorsed—Distances to Ohio, 1754.

---

[81] Georges Creek is identified as *"Lonaconina"* Creek on Benjamin Winslow's 1736 map, which is titled **"Plan of the upper part of Potomack River called Cohongorooto. Survey'd in the year 1736."** Only a short section of the creek at present-day Westernport is illustrated on the map.

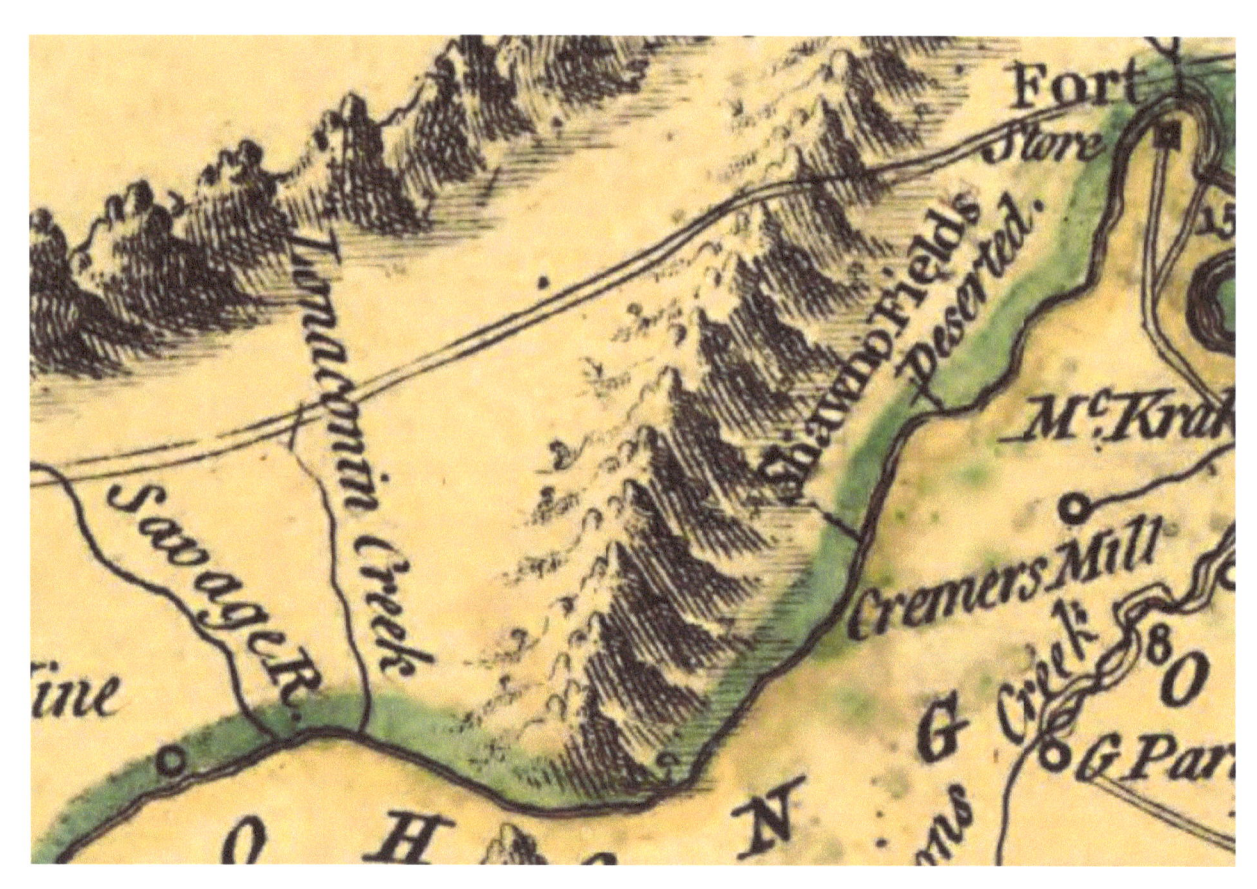

Figure 14— This portion of the 1755 Fry and Jefferson map illustrates the road westward from Fort Cumberland as passing through the headwaters of Georges (Lonaconin) Creek (Library of Congress Call No. G3880 1755 .F72). The road was added to the map on January 1, 1755, well in advance of Braddock's expedition.

9. Participant expedition maps

Introduction to the four maps that are discussed in more detail below

The four maps described below are attributed to key participants of Braddock's expedition. All four show the location of Braddock's second camp as being located between the head forks of Georges Creek. Two of the maps are by the same author, Christopher Gist. The other two are attributed to Harry Gordon and Robert Orme, and are referred to hereafter as the *"Gordon map"* and the *"Orme map"*, respectively. Several printed versions of the *"Orme map"* are included.

One of Gist's maps and the *"Orme map"* show the headwaters of Braddock Run as consisting of two forks, one flowing southeasterly, and the other flowing northeasterly. The two head forks are most easily interpreted as Porter Run and Preston Run, or representing Porter Run and a combination of ½-mile of Preston Run and the tributary that follows Hoffman Hollow. These two maps are most easily interpreted as showing Braddock's road as following Porter Run to or toward the village of Eckhart Mines.

One of Gist's maps and the *"Gordon map"* show the headwaters of Braddock Run as consisting of three head forks joining at essentially the same place. The *"Gordon map"*, seems to represent Porter Run and its headwaters extremely well, including courses and compass bearings, with one of the headwaters being the northerly running stream that flows down through Washington Hollow.

The representation of the three streams are very schematic on the Gist map, and are not easily interpreted. One basis for interpreting the illustration of these three streams is to believe that they represent the same three streams that are shown in excellent detail on the *"Gordon map"*. Another basis for interpreting the illustrations of these three streams is their proximity to one another. There are two places on Porter Run where the mouths of tributaries are no more than 1/10th of a mile (176 yards) apart, and in one these two places the mouths of the respective valleys are nearly directly across from one another, with one of the valleys being Washington Hollow. By comparison, the mouth of the Preston Run tributary that follows Hoffman Hollow is fully ½-mile (873 yards) from the mouth of Porter Run. On these bases, I suspect that the joining of the three streams on the Gist map also represents the headwaters of Porter Run at the village of Eckhart Mines. Given the highly schematic nature of the Gist map, however, I concede that the three head streams it illustrates could possibly be interpreted as representing Porter Run, Preston Run, and the tributary that follows Hoffman Hollow. One count against this interpretation is that physically, Porter Run is simply a seamless continuation of Braddock Run. There is no physical reason to view Porter Run as being anything different from Braddock Run In other words, by all appearances, the main stream simply receives the waters of Preston Run at Clarysville.

None of the participant maps even remotely suggest that Braddock's expedition made a hard right-hand turn at the top of Hoffman Hollow to follow the valley of Georges Creek northward to the second camp. Likewise, none of the maps even remotely suggest the second camp was located east of Georges Creek.

Gist's maps of Braddock's expedition

Christopher Gist participated in Braddock's expedition,[82] and produced two contemporaneous maps of the route (Figure 15).[83] Braddock's route covered ground that Gist was obviously very familiar with, having explored the area in 1751, having participated in opening the Ohio Company road, having guided George Washington along the road in 1753, having participated in Braddock's 1755 expedition, and having two homes along the road — one at Wills Creek, and another at the site of present-day Mount Braddock, Pennsylvania. He was definitely on his home turf.

The relevant portion of Gist's September 15, 1755 map, titled "**The Draught of Genl. Braddocks Route towards Fort DuQuesne as deliver'd to Capt. McKeller Engineer**" is included at the top of Figure 15.[84] As noted above, I suspect that this map illustrates the three head streams of Porter Run coming together at the village of Eckhart Mines.

Using this interpretation, the map shows Braddock's road following Braddock Run to Porter Run, and then following the central branch of Porter Run for some distance before turning generally west to the camp at Martin's. In other words, the interpretation is harmonious with the theory that Braddock's road ran through the village of Eckhart Mines. The map also clearly shows the second camp, at Martin's plantation, as being located between the head forks of Georges Creek.

Gist's other map, included at the bottom of Figure 15, seems to show Porter and Preston runs, seems to show Braddock's expedition following Porter Run, and clearly shows the second camp as being located between the head forks of Georges Creek. The two Gist maps are obviously highly schematic; look at the randomly drawn representations of Braddock Run between Wills Creek and the site of Clarysville. Although these two maps do provide some support for the theory presented herein, I doubt that anyone would try to use either map as evidence that Braddock made a hard right-hand turn toward Martin's plantation after exiting Hoffman Hollow, or use either map as evidence that the second camp was located east of Georges Creek.

I view waterways on early maps, and their valleys, as one of the critical things early travelers used for orientation. When aligned with the direction of travel, the valleys of these waterways provided passage through mountainous terrain. When not, they served as mileposts, and the larger waterways were obstacles that had to be crossed at passable fording sites. For this reason, I don't view stream depictions on early maps as mere trivialities.

---

[82] Many secondary sources state that Gist served as a guide during Braddock's expedition. I have not attempted to identify the basis of these statements.

[83] In his 2013 book "**Braddock's Road: Mapping the British Expedition...**", Norman L. Baker refers to Gist's map work as the Rosetta Stone for present-day individuals researching Braddock's road and camp sites. In his preface, Mr. Baker indicates that Gist's maps of the expedition were unknown at the time of the research performed by Atkinson and Lacock.

[84] The existence of one of Gist's maps was identified by Robert L. Bantz.

Gordon's 1755 map of Braddock's expedition is at the core of the Porter Run theory

Like one of Gist's maps, a map commonly attributed to Engineer[85] Harry Gordon[86] (Figure 16) illustrates three streams coming together, and shows the second camp as being located more or less due west of the confluence of the three streams, and between the head branches of Georges Creek. The original map, which is located at the Royal Library, is unsigned but is suspected to be the map referenced in a letter Gordon wrote on July 23, 1755. To be consistent with other historical writings, this anonymous map is referenced herein to as the *"Gordon map"*.

The appearance of the three streams coming together seems to be an excellent match to both the courses and compass bearings of the head streams of Porter Run at the village of Eckhart Mines, with the northerly flowing branch following Washington Hollow. Likewise, the illustration of Georges Creek includes a tributary of each head branch that seem to match to tributaries that are located in the environs of Frostburg. Based on such detail — which differs markedly from Gist's maps — the location of the second camp does not appear to haphazardly drawn.

In addition to sometimes showing the route of Braddock's road as a dotted line, the *"Gordon map"* highlights the route with white space. The route indicated by the white highlighting heads more or less due west after leaving the joining of the three streams. This map is obviously schematic in nature, but it fits the theory of the book extremely well. At the same time, I don't think anyone would attempt to use it as evidence that Braddock made a hard right-hand turn toward Martin's plantation after exiting Hoffman Hollow, or to use it as evidence that the second camp was located east of Georges Creek.

One might attempt to interpret the *"Gordon map"* as providing a truly horrible representation of the valleys of Porter Run, Preston Run, and the tributary that follows Hoffman Hollow, and illustrating Braddock's route as following Hoffman Hollow and then heading west on Middleton's projected course. The illustrated forks of Georges Creek might then be interpreted as being Winebrenner Run and Georges Creek. One serious problem with this interpretation is that the mouth of the Hoffman Hollow tributary is fully ½-mile from the mouth of Porter Run; they do not join together at nearly the same place. Another problem with this interpretation is that it does not include the traditional route of Braddock's road through Frostburg — a route that is mentioned by a 1793 road-related law that is quoted later in this book. Another issue is that the compass bearings of the three streams that join together do not match the bearings (and proximities) of Porter Run, Preston Run, and the Hoffman Hollow tributary nearly as well as they match those of the head branches of Porter Run — where the valleys of two of the head streams are located nearly opposite one another. Because the streams match the headwaters of Porter Run so well, I vastly prefer that interpretation of the confluence of the three streams on the *"Gordon map"*.

The *"Gordon map"* is badly out of scale, but the cartographer's sense of compass direction, as depicted by the orientation of the mountains, and the orientation of Braddock Run below the first camp are good. With that in mind, it seems preposterous to interpret the southerly course of

---

[85] According to Hanna's 1911 book "**The Wilderness Trail**", Harry Gordon was an engineer associated with Braddock's campaign.
[86] This copy of the map, a reproduction, was provided by Robert L. Bantz.

Braddock Run below the joining of the three streams as anything but Porter Run. Furthermore, Gordon's map depicts the curved route across Savage Mountain that modern researchers have documented. With this curve detail in mind, why doesn't the *"Gordon map"* illustrate Lacock's abrupt right-hand turn at the top of Hoffman Hollow?

The *"Gordon map"* includes the statement, *"The Courses of the Waters are taken from a Sketch of Mr Gists. The Road being full of short windings, the different Bearings of it could not be expressed, but the general Bearings are pretty just. The mountainous Ridges are expressed in Greater perspective, and the hard pinch's of Hills in plan. The Springs are expressed with a Dot in water Colour."* The map includes a tabular *"Abstract of a Journal"* that includes descriptions of roadwork and the camps that are clearly based on Gordon's journal. This helps to identify Gordon as the author of the map. The more detailed depictions of Georges Creek and Braddock Run suggest that Gordon did not simply copy Gist's map in the vicinity of Clarysville. For example, the *"Gordon map"* correctly shows Porter Run flowing south-southeast to the easterly turn at the site of Clarysville and correctly shows the broad valley of Preston Run and the course of the Hoffman Hollow tributary west-southwest of that turn, and although badly out of scale, correctly shows Braddock Run flowing generally east from the site of Clarysville to the turn at the first camp, and correctly illustrates the valley that is located and oriented south-southwest of the first camp between Dans Mountain and Piney Mountain, and then correctly shows Braddock Run flowing north-northeast after the turn at the first camp. Between the first camp and the site of Clarysville, the map even correctly shows the rounded shape of the northern end of Dans Mountain (view the shape on LIDAR). For additional information, see Figure 17, which is the most important figure of this book.

When compared to the topographical map of Figure 1, the head streams of the eastern head fork of Georges Creek seem incorrect on the *"Gordon map"*. Figure 18 is a late 1800s map[87] that shows the head streams in more detail, demonstrating the basis for the head stream representation on the *"Gordon map"*.

The details on the *"Gordon map"* are a compelling reason to suspect that Braddock's forces followed Porter Run to the site of the present-day village of Eckhart Mines. The map is just too detailed to believe that what looks like, and is oriented like, Porter Run is just a horribly bad illustration of Braddock Run. Even though it is badly out of scale, the *"Gordon map"* is simply too accurate in terms of compass bearings to believe that Gordon misrepresented Braddock Run as flowing south-southeast between the first camp and the site of Clarysville. In my opinion, the joining of the three streams has to represent the site of the village of Eckhart Mines.

Orme's map of Braddock's expedition

Robert Orme was aide-de-camp to General Edward Braddock,[88] and participated in Braddock's expedition against Fort Duquesne. A map (Figure 19) that is commonly attributed to Orme, and

---

[87] This map was identified by Lynn Groesbeck Bowman.
[88] According to Volume VI of the "**Minutes of the Provincial Council of Pennsylvania**", Robert Orme was an aide to General Braddock. Orme was wounded at Braddock's defeat, and wrote a letter to Governor Sharpe from Fort Cumberland on July 18, 1755 describing the July 9, 1755 battle.

titled *"Map of the Country between Wills Creek and Fort du Quesne"* accompanied an article titled *"Account of the Establishment of Fort Du Quesne"* that was published in the December, 1758 issue of "**The Gentleman's and London Magazine**".[89] The *"Orme map"* was also published in the January 1759 issue of "**The Grand Magazine of Universal Intelligence and Monthly Chronicle of Our Times**"; see Figure 20.

The depiction of *"Three Forks"* (Turkeyfoot) is very similar to one of the maps attributed to Gist, and it seems clear that one of the maps influenced the other. Figure 21 includes more of the September 15, 1755 Gist map that is included at the top of Figure 15, so that it can be compared to the *"Orme map"* of Figure 19 and Figure 20. Figure 22 shows more of the Gist map that is included at the bottom of Figure 15, so it can be compared to Figure 21.

The 1758 *"Orme map"* (Figure 19) clearly and unambiguously shows the route of Braddock's road following Porter Run to or at least toward the village of Eckhart Mines, and then shows the route turning west-southwest to the second camp — and shows the second camp as being located within the head forks of Georges Creek. Whether this depiction is accurate or not, the *"Orme map"* doesn't provide any support for the idea that Braddock made a hard right-hand turn up the valley of Georges Creek and toward the site of Grahamtown after exiting Hoffman Hollow. It also doesn't provide any support for the conventional wisdom concerning the location of the second camp.

A 1758 color version of the *"Orme map"* that is titled "**A map of the country between Will's Creek & Monongahela River shewing the rout and encampments of the English army in 1755**" was published by Thomas Jefferys, and is included at the top of Figure 23 and used as the cover of this book. This version[90] of the *"Orme map"* also shows Braddock's road following Porter Run. Winthrop Sargent's 1855 book "**The History of an Expedition against fort Du Quesne, in 1755…**" includes an unfaithful reproduction of the map that fails to accurately replicate Braddock's route in the vicinity of the head forks of Braddock Run. This version is shown at the bottom of Figure 23.

Summary of the evidence from the participant maps

None of the participant maps even remotely suggest that Braddock's expedition followed the valley of Georges Creek northward from the top of Hoffman Hollow. Gist's maps, the *"Gordon map"*, and the *"Orme map"* all seem to show Braddock's road departing westward from the waters

---

[89] This map and article were identified by Richard C. Sloop, who owns an original copy of the magazine they are printed in. According to 25506.01 of John W. Docktor's "**Cartobibliography of Pennsylvania Maps Prior to 1800**", a collection at the Library of Congress that is titled "**United States French & Indian War Pennsylvania (Braddock's March formation of Line) 1755**" includes a photocopy of a manuscript version of the *"Orme map"* that is titled "**A Map of the County between Wills Creek & Monongahela River shewing the rout & Encampments of the English Army in 1755**". According to Docktor, the original manuscript map is housed at the British Library (Kings Manuscript No. 212), and includes latitude and longitude lines on its margins.

[90] This color map is also included in Thomas Jefferys' 1768 book "**A general topography of North America and the West Indies. Being a collection of all the maps, charts, plans, and particular surveys, that have been published of that part of the world, either in Europe or America**." The 1768 version has a hand-inked plate number in the upper right-hand corner, and the version included as Figure 21 does not. Volume 2 of the 1869 book "**A Dictionary of Books Relating to America…**", by Sabin, et al, describes the folio version of the map that is included herein as Figure 21, and is the basis for the 1758 date I use.

of Braddock Run at the headwaters of Porter Run in the vicinity of the village of Eckhart Mines. To me, the consistency of what these maps depict outweighs the argument that one should not interpret the route between Clarysville and Frostburg literally in view of the schematic nature of the maps. Aside from that, the *"Gordon map"* does such a beautiful job of representing the way Porter Run continues on seamlessly as Braddock Run at Clarysville, that I simply have to accept the route it illustrates between the village of Eckhart Mines and Frostburg.

I've encountered the same sort of argument regarding the location of Braddock's second camp. The argument goes something like this: One should not assume that the location depicted on the maps is accurate, in view of the highly schematic nature of the maps. The aforementioned maps are indeed schematic, but *every single one of them* indicates that the site of the second camp was located west of Georges Creek. What a huge coincidence if they all happen to be wrong!

Let's face reality: Even though the maps are crude, it would not be too difficult for each map author to draw the camp at Martin's on the correct side of the line representing Georges Creek — if he knew where the camp at Martin's was located. British Regulars Gordon and Orme, who participated in Braddock's expedition, may have had enough time to become familiar with the location of Martin's plantation while staying at Fort Cumberland before the expedition.[91] If they didn't, this was only the second camp of the expedition, and even though the locations of the rest of the camps might have become blurred in their memory, surely the locations of the first two camps did not. As for Gist, who opened the road the expedition followed, it is simply comical to argue that he lacked the knowledge or the ability to draw the camp at Martin's correctly in relation to the head forks of Georges Creek.

---

[91] Martin's plantation was known to at least some of the members of Braddock's army prior to the expedition. An entry in Braddock's orderly book for May 15, 1755, written from Fort Cumberland, includes the statement, *"One subaltern, one sergt 1 corpl and 30 centl to march this evening to Mr. Martin's where the troop of Light Horse graze, the men to take tents with them and provisions for three days, the officer to receive his orders from Captain Stuart of the Light Horse; this guard to be relievd every 3d Day."* (**"History of Cumberland"**, Lowdermilk, 1878.)

Reconsidering Braddock's Road to Martin's

Figure 15 — The color image above is from Christopher Gist's 1755 manuscript map of Braddock's road. The image below is another version[92] of Gist's map that shows a different representation of the headwaters of Braddock Run, with Braddock's road more clearly following Porter Run. Both maps illustrate the second camp as being located between the head forks of Georges Creek. Gist's maps cannot be viewed as giving the precise course of Braddock's expedition, because one illustrates the route as heading northwest from the headwaters of Braddock Run to the second camp, while the other illustrates the route as heading slightly west-southwest from the headwaters of Braddock Run to the second camp.

---

[92] Norman L. Baker reports that there were two authentic versions of Gist's map. The bottom version of one of Gist's maps was provided by Robert L. Bantz.

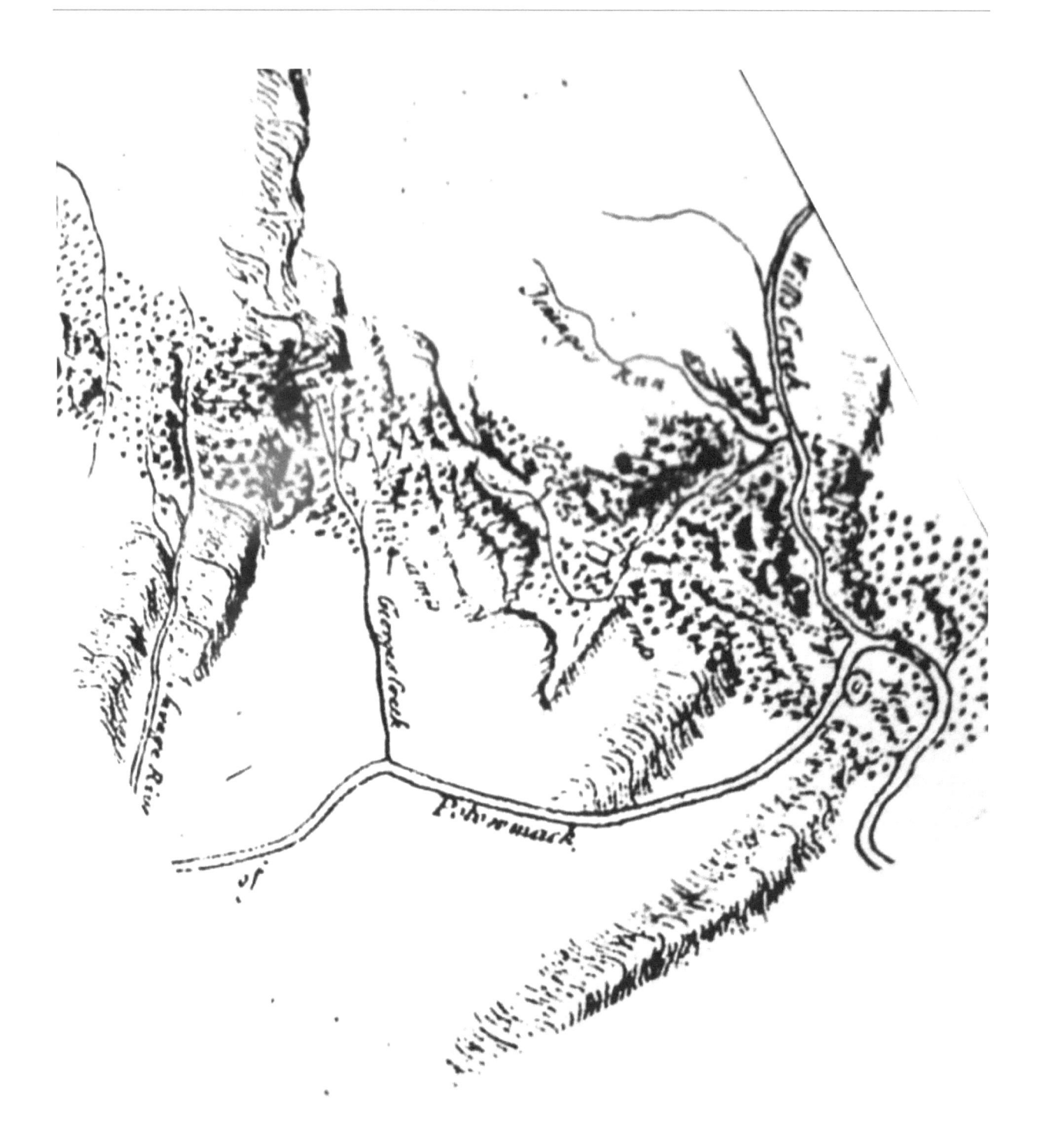

Figure 16 — This is from the *"Gordon map"* of Braddock's road. It indicates that Braddock's expedition followed Porter Run, and illustrates the second camp as being located between the head forks of Georges Creek. One interesting detail on this map is a stockade encircling the Ohio Company's New Store.

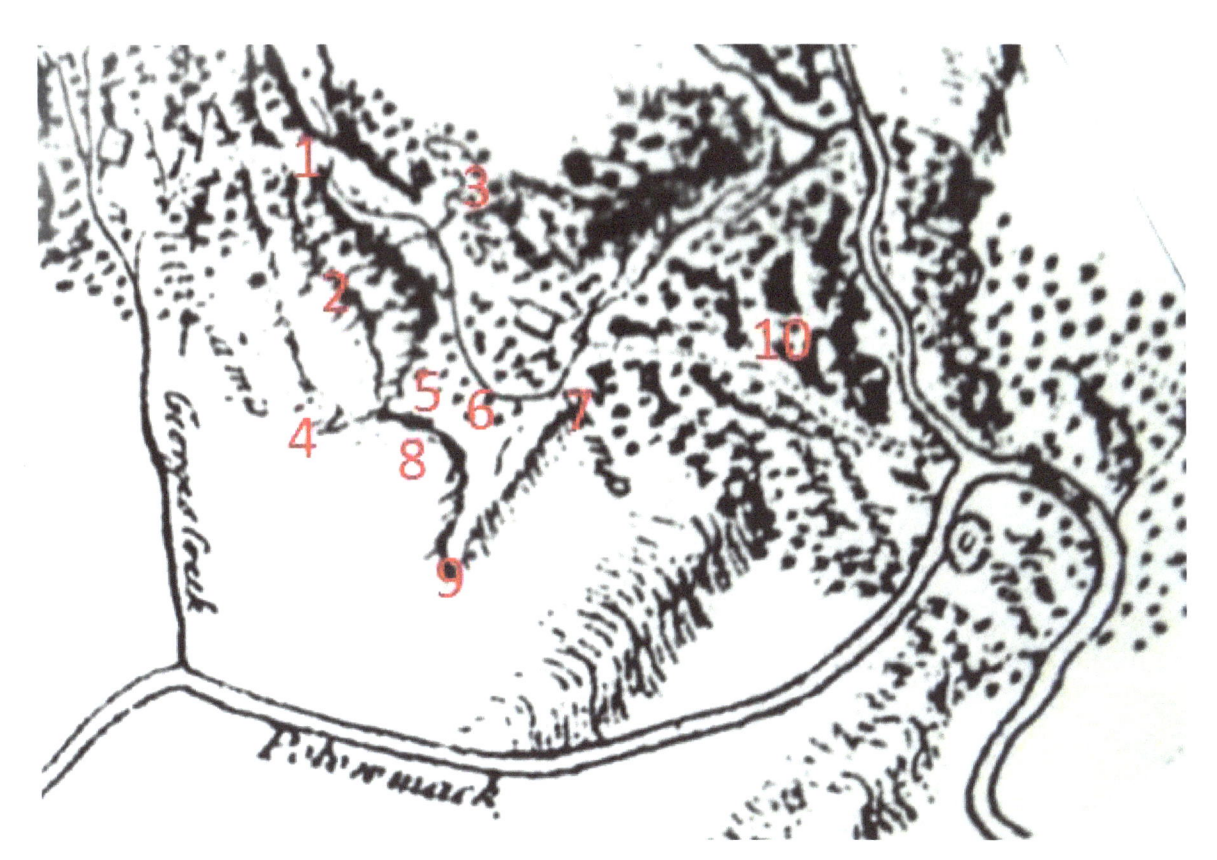

Figure 17 — The *"Gordon map"* is out of scale, but the bearings are excellent. I have been told that Gordon miss-illustrated the turn in Braddock Run at the first camp, drawing that turn as nearly 180 degrees, copying Gist but making the squiggly representation of Braddock Run on Gist's maps even worse. I disagree, and believe that the distance between the turn at the first camp and Clarysville is simply out of scale. Looking at the numbers on the map, the stream at 1 is near where the Old National Pike comes out on Route 36. The stream at 2 follows Washington Hollow. The stream at 3 is now followed by Piney Mountain Road. The Hoffman Hollow tributary is shown at 4. The broad valley at Clarysville is shown at 5. The mouth of Porter Run at Clarysville is shown at 6 as it really exists – a continuous smooth bend in Braddock Run that hugs the mountain closely. The turn in Braddock Run at Allegany Grove is shown at 7. The rounded northern end of Dans Mountain is shown at 8 (look at the mountain on a LIDAR map to see this shape). The valley between Haystack Mountain and Dans Mountain is shown at 9. This map even shows the slight bend in Braddock's road across Haystack Mountain at 10. With this level of detail, it seems hard to believe that Gordon would have failed to include Lacock's radical right-hand turn at the top of Hoffman Hollow. This map shows the waterways in exquisite detail, and when viewed in the context of the Walnutt Levill survey, tells us that Braddock followed the Ohio Company road between the village of Eckhart Mines and the second camp. With this map and Orme's journal, it becomes clear that Braddock's second camp was located a quarter mile east of Sand Spring Run, where Robert Kenney found a cannonball and other artifacts.

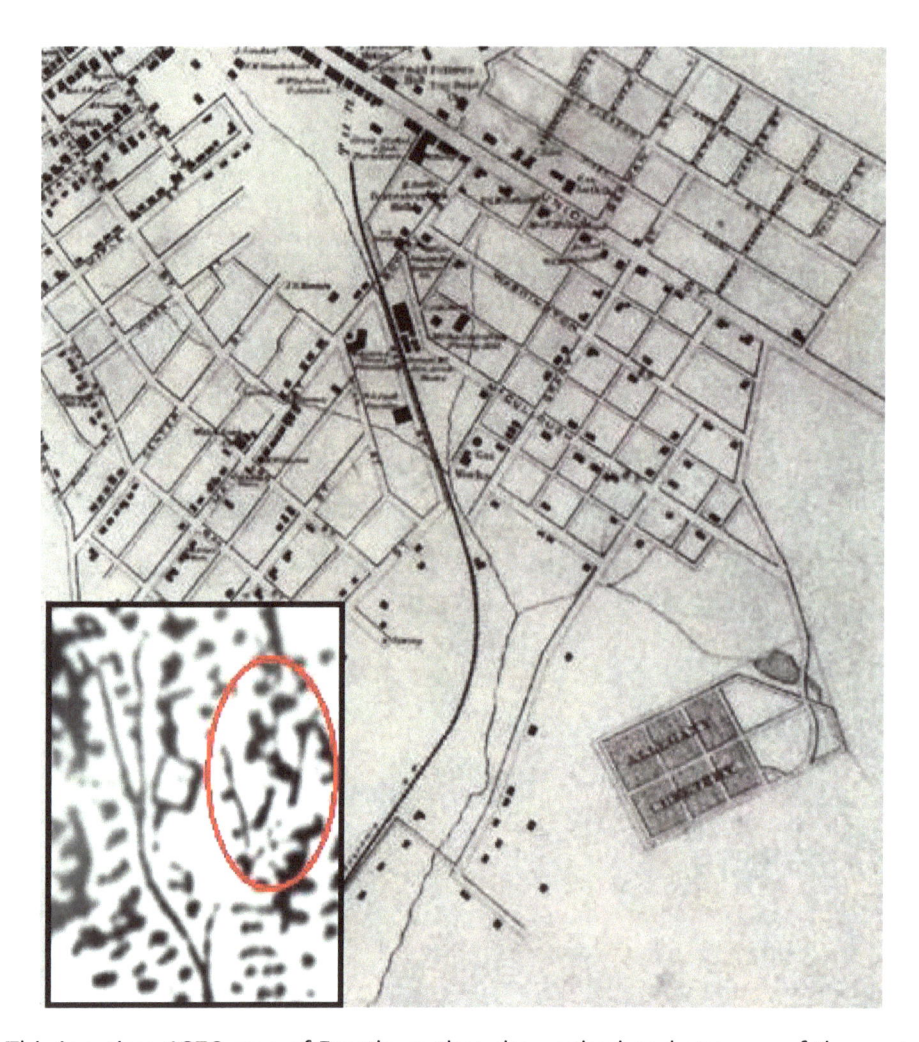

Figure 18 — This is a circa 1876 map of Frostburg that shows the head streams of the eastern head fork of Georges Creek. The inset is from the *"Gordon map"*, and Gordon's representation of the head streams of the eastern fork are circled. This comparison shows that there were several southerly flowing head streams in the area, including one that flows into the head stream that encircles the Allegany Cemetery. In other words, the head stream representation on the *"Gordon map"* depicts actual head streams, but does not include every head stream. One might speculate that Gordon only sketched the head streams the expedition crossed or were in very close proximity to.

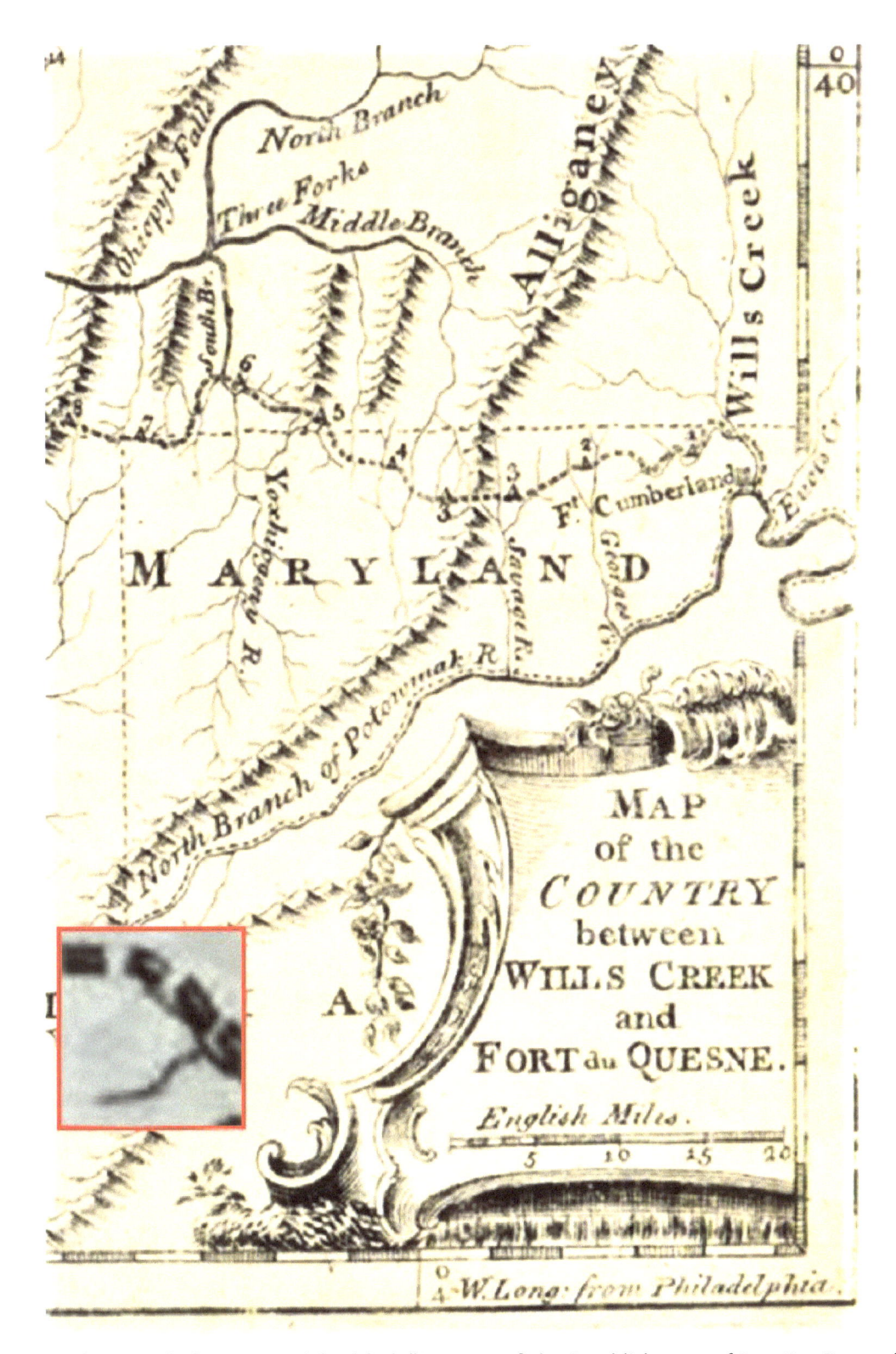

Figure 19 — This map is from an article titled *"Account of the Establishment of Fort Du Quesne"* in the December, 1758 issue of **"The Gentleman's and London Magazine"**, and shows Braddock's road following Porter Run. This map is commonly attributed to Robert Orme, but the depiction of *"Three Forks"* (Turkeyfoot) is very similar to one of the maps attributed to Gist. The inset is enlarged, for more detail.

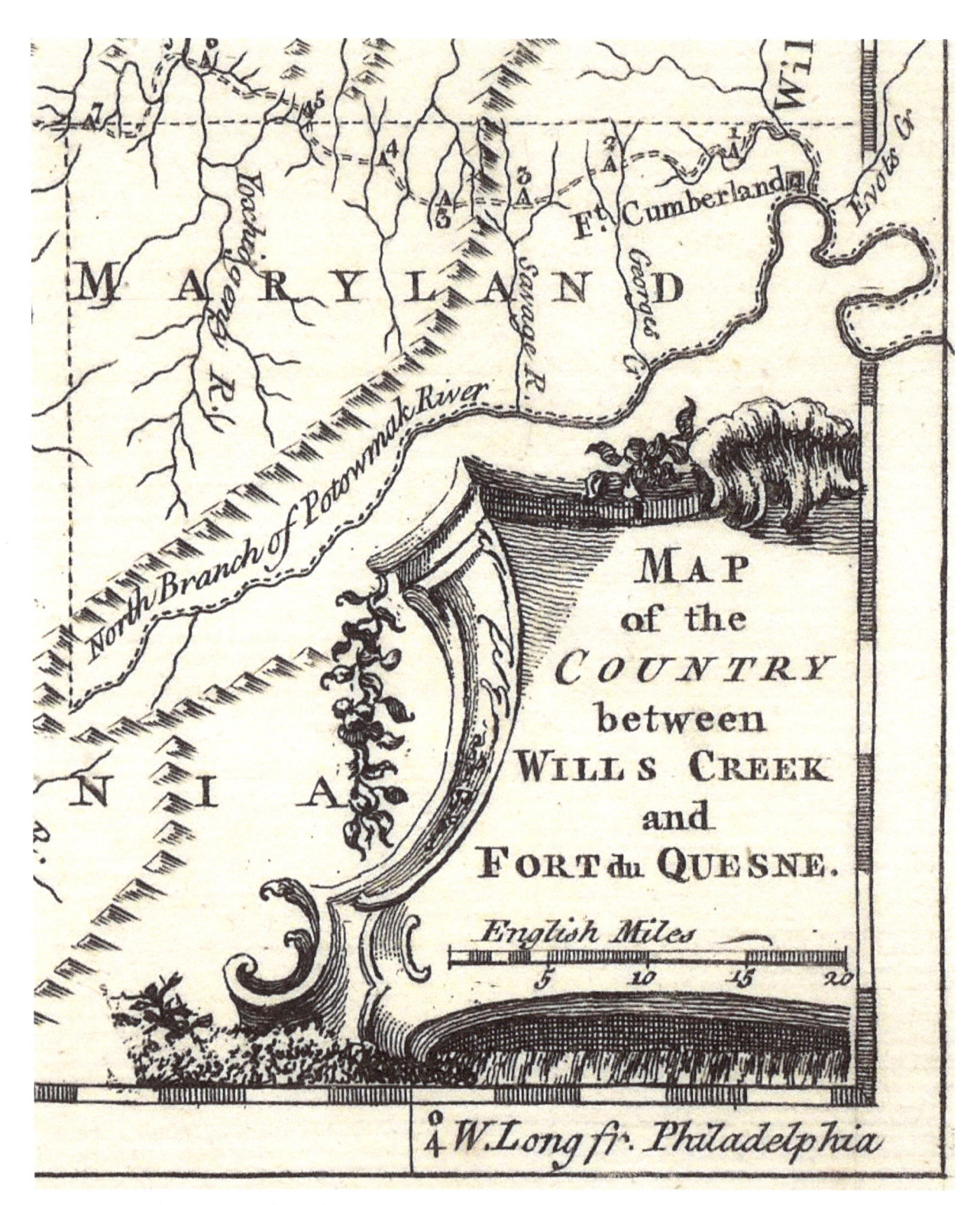

Figure 20 — This version of the *"Orme map"* is from the January, 1759 issue of "**The Grand Magazine of Universal Intelligence and Monthly Chronicle of Our Times**". There are small differences from the 1758 version of Figure 19, such as the lack of a period after the word *"Philadelphia"*. See if you can spot other differences. The map illustrates two locations for the third camp, which historians view as correct.

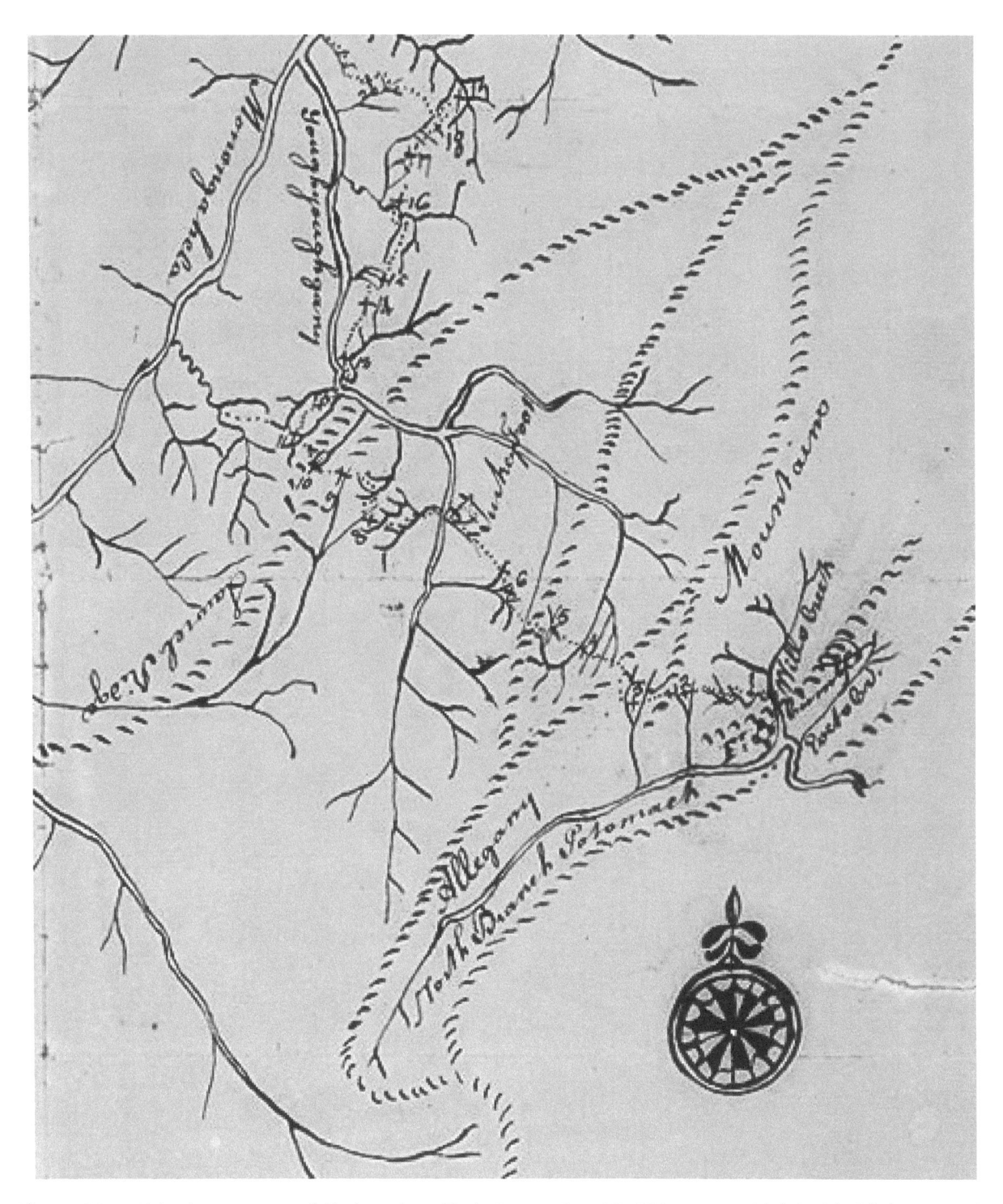

Figure 21 — This shows more of Christopher Gist's September 15, 1755 map, which is titled "**The Draught of Genl. Braddocks Route towards Fort DuQuesne as deliver'd to Capt. McKeller Engineer**". This image is provided so that the reader can compare the depiction of Turkeyfoot on this map to the 1758 "**Map of the Country between Wills Creek and Fort du Quesne**" that is included as Figure 19.

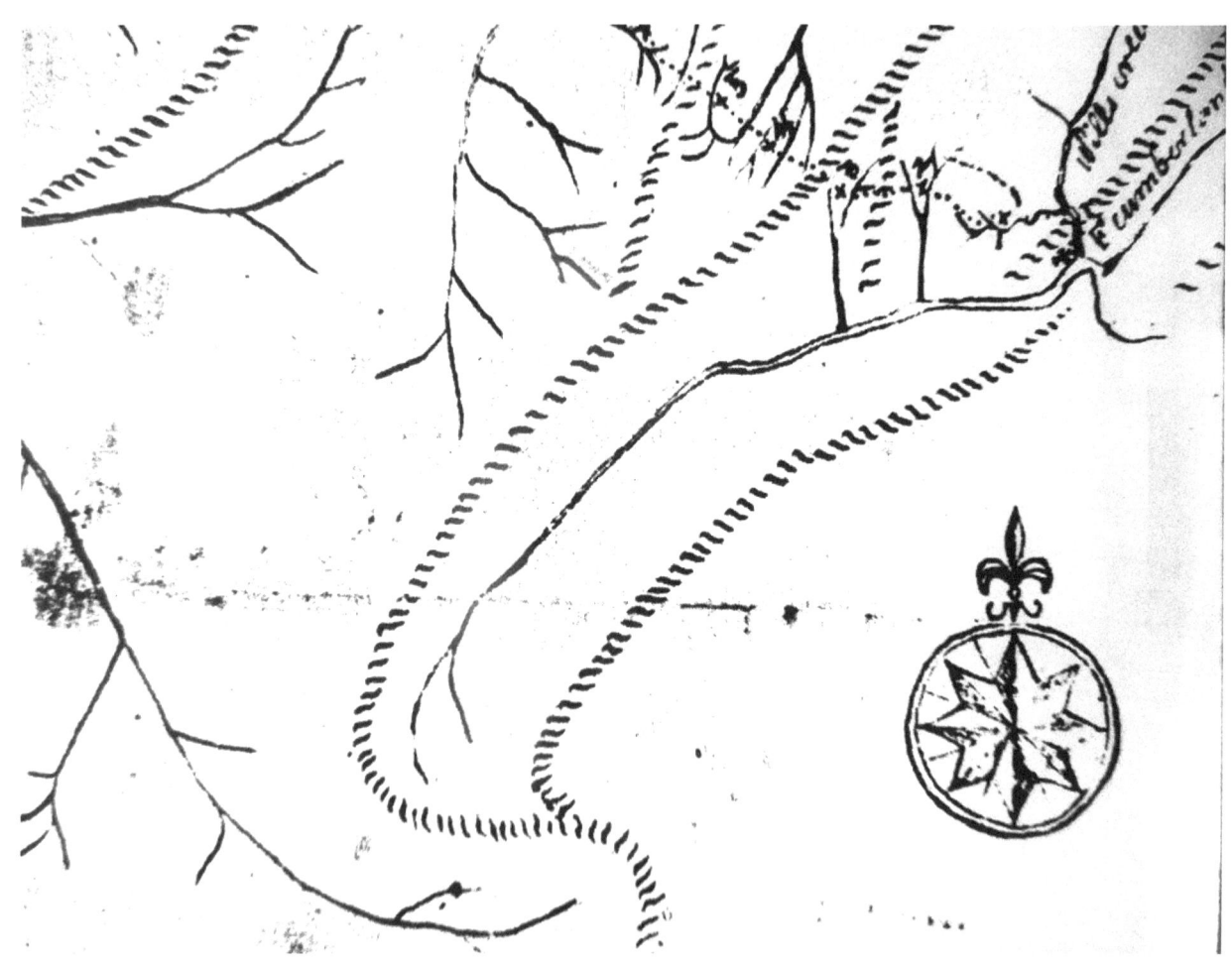

Figure 22 — This shows more of the Gist map that is included at the bottom of Figure 15, so it can be compared to Figure 21.

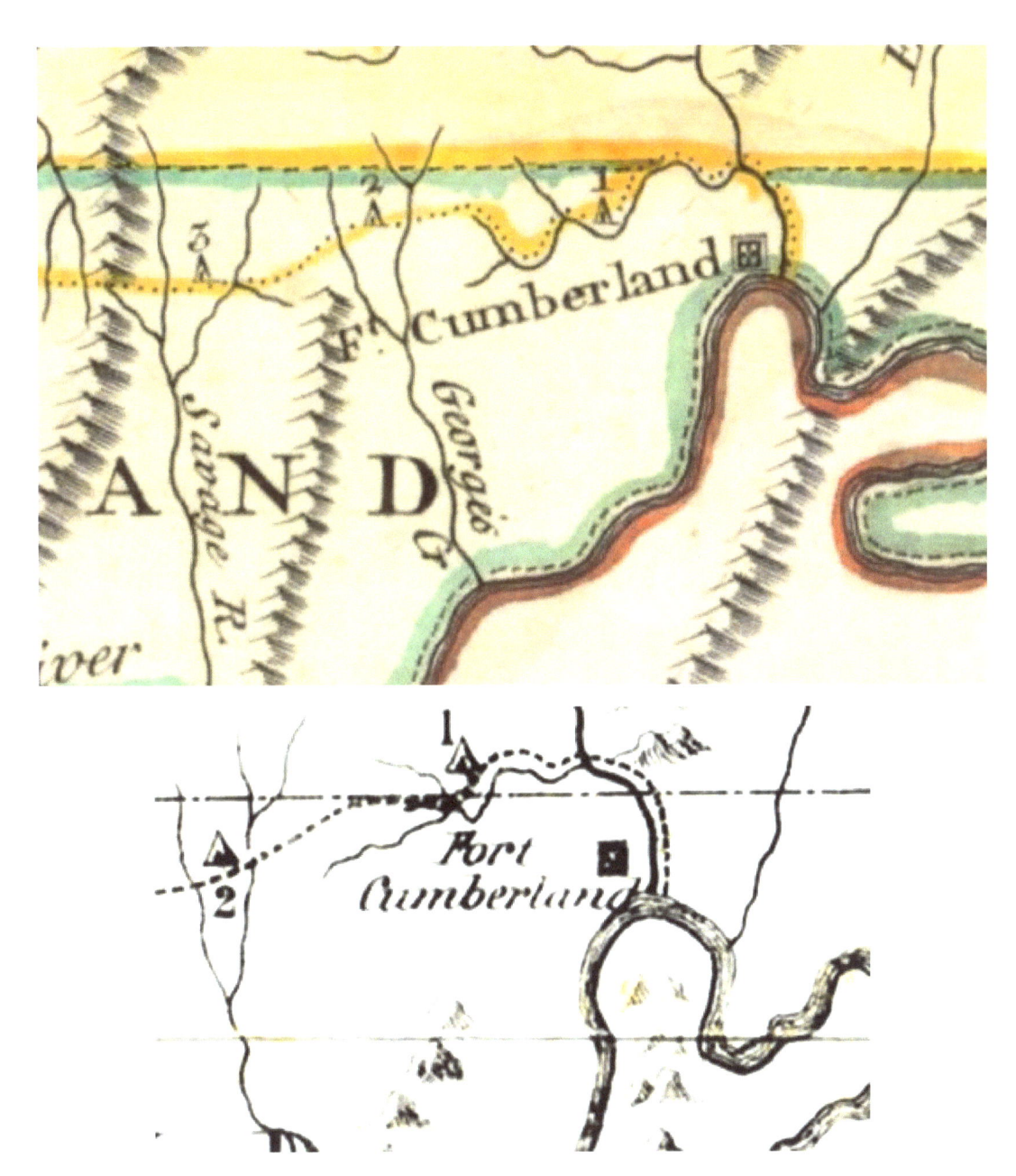

Figure 23 — The color image above is from a version of the *"Orme map"* that was engraved by Thomas Jefferys and published as part of a folio of six Braddock expedition-related maps in 1758. The map is titled **"A map of the country between Will's Creek & Monongahela River shewing the rout and encampments of the English army in 1755"**. This map clearly shows Braddock's road following Porter Run. The black and white image below is from an unfaithful but widely distributed copy of the *"Orme map"* that does not show Braddock's road following Porter Run. Rather than indicating something profound, this lower map is just a sloppy reproduction.

10. Subsequent mid-1700s maps

Introduction

This Chapter includes maps that were made several years after Braddock's expedition.

A 1758 map informs us to use caution with maps made after the expedition

Figure 24 is from a map that is marked July 12, 1758, and is titled *"Military Sketch from Philadelphia to Fort Du Quesne"*.[93] The illustration of Turkeyfoot (not included on Figure 24) is like the depiction on Christopher Gist's September 15, 1755 map and the *"Orme map"*, indicating that it was influenced by one of those maps. The map covers much of Pennsylvania, showing many waterways, roads, and paths. It includes a numbered table of the camps from Braddock's expedition, and erroneously illustrates the Georges Creek camp within the watershed of the Youghiogheny River. The map is included in this book to show just how wrong large area maps can be when it comes to details the author is unfamiliar with. One can certainly observe, however, that this map definitely locates the second camp west of the eastern head fork of Georges Creek!

A circa-1759/60 manuscript map showing the road to Martin's plantation and beyond

The relevant portion of an anonymous schematic manuscript map that is located at the Library of Congress[94] is included as Figure 25. This map would probably be from circa-1759/60, because it identifies the location of Burd's fort at Redstone. Like Gist's maps, this manuscript map appears to illustrate Braddock's road as following Porter Run, the northern head fork of Braddock run. This map illustrates Martin's plantation as being on the west side of a main branch of Georges Creek, where other maps locate Braddock's second camp. This map is obviously highly schematic, but at the same time, I don't think anyone will be using it as evidence that Braddock made a hard right-hand turn toward Martin's plantation after exiting Hoffman Hollow, or will use it as evidence that the second camp was located east of Georges Creek.

Although very schematic in nature, the map includes a straight dashed line that illustrates the route of Braddock's road as traveling west-southwest between the head forks of Braddock Run and Martin's plantation, which is harmonious with the theory presented herein. When such straight-line representations of roads appear on maps, however, about the most they can be interpreted as indicating is where a particular section of road begins and ends. This straight line begins on Porter Run, and ends on Georges Creek, a little north of Martin's house.

One argument I have encountered concerning the location of Martin's plantation on Figure 25 is that the eastern head fork of Georges Creek has a small northward-flowing tributary that partially encircles the Grahamtown and Allegany Cemetery area where conventional wisdom locates the second camp, and this tributary may be what is illustrated. That tributary is shown on Figure 1. I sincerely doubt that the map of Figure 25 illustrates a small tributary of Georges Creek, and ignores the main eastern (and southerly flowing) fork of Georges Creek that originates near Taylor Street

---

[93] The photo of this map was provided by Dan Press, and was taken at the British Archives.
[94] Library of Congress G3821.S26 1760 .B7, titled *"Case C No 1"*, from the Peter Force map collection.

and the bend in the National Pike. In any case, the argument simply does hold up against the illustration of the head forks, and the location of the second camp, on the *"Gordon map"* (Figure 16).

Three versions of a circa-1760 map showing the road to Martin's plantation

Figure 26, Figure 27, and Figure 28 are from three different versions of the same basic map, and all three are from the British National Archives.[95] Figure 26 was prepared by Engineer Elias Meyer. A tattered fragment of paper is glued to the back of Figure 26.[96] It carries a conspicuous broad red arrow stamp, and includes the description, *"United States — Rivers Monongahella, Youghiogany, Allegeny, & French; showing Forts Ptt, Venango, & Le Beuf.* The inclusion of the word *"United States"* indicates that the description was written long after the map was made. The fragment of paper also includes, *"Lt. Col. Eyre 1 Dec 1760. X 7/3"*.

All three versions of the map illustrate Martin's residence[97] as being located west of the eastern head fork of Georges Creek. All three maps clearly illustrate Preston Run and Porter Run. Unfortunately, all three of the maps use straight lines to represent the road between Wills Creek and Martin's plantation. Because of this, nothing can be gleaned from the maps concerning the route of the road. Taken literally, which would be unwise considering the ruler-straight lines, some might argue that the maps support Lackock's Hoffman Hollow route. They do not.

Shippen's "Draught of The Monongahela & Youghiogany Rivers"

Figure 29 is a map from Hulbert's 1903 book "**The Old Glade (Forbes's) Road**" Hulbert describes it as Shippen's[98] November, 1759 "**Draught of The Monongahela & Youghiogany Rivers**". Hulbert has obviously added some printed text, to clarify difficult-to-read cursive text. Examined closely, Figure 29 is virtually identical to the maps included as Figure 26, Figure 27, and Figure 28, down to the last molehill. Clearly, one of the maps is the basis for the others.

Like Figure 26, Figure 27, and Figure 28, Hulbert's map illustrates Martin's plantation as being on the west side of some part of Georges Creek — if one interprets Georges Creek as being represented by the wavy vertical line that is located east of Martin's, and is drawn at an angle to, and passes through the repetitive squiggly lines that represent mountains. Like Figure 26, Figure 27, and Figure 28, Hulbert's map illustrates Preston Run and Porter Run, although one hill is

---

[95] The photos included as Figure 26, Figure 27, and Figure 28 were provided by Dan Press, who took them at the British National Archives.

[96] This is the recollection of Dan Press, and his recollection appears to be confirmed by an online description provided by the British National Archives (Reference: MPHH, 1/346 Former reference: X/7/3). From the British National Archives description of a report that accompanies the map, it seems clear that Eyre endorsed the map and the report on December 1, 1760.

[97] James Kenny's June 1, 1763 journal entry describes staying at a house on Georges Creek, as follows, *"This night it was so Cold at ye House by George's Creek we thot there was frost."*

[98] A September 1, 1759 letter Bouquet wrote to Edward Shippen from Fort Bedford includes the following statement: *"Colonel Burd & Col Shippen are gone to Fort Cumberland, to open a new Road to the Mouth of Red Stone Creek, and build Storehouses upon The Mononghehela; being at last obliged to have recourse to Virginia to avoid the Impending Ruin of the Army."*

located so close to the confluence of Preston and Porter runs that it almost looks like a third waterway. Like Figure 26, Figure 27, and Figure 28, Hulbert's map uses straight lines to represent the road between Wills Creek and Martin's plantation. Because of this, nothing can be gleaned from Hulbert's map concerning the route of the road.

Comparing Hulbert's map to one of the maps from the British Archives

Figure 30 is a view of more of *"the black Fort Cumberland map"* that is included as Figure 27. Figure 31 is a view of more of the Hulbert map that is included as Figure 29. These figures are included so the reader can verify that the maps of Figure 26, Figure 27, and Figure 28 are virtually identical to the Hulbert map.

Conclusion

One of the maps (Figure 25) indicates that Martin's residence was located west of some part of Georges Creek. Another other map, included here in four variations, indicates that Martin's residence was located between the head forks of Georges Creek, and indicates that the road crossed the head forks. Both maps indicate that Martin's residence was located south of the road. A third map (Figure 24) does not include Martin's residence, but does show the road crossing the head forks of Georges Creek.

Reconsidering Braddock's Road to Martin's

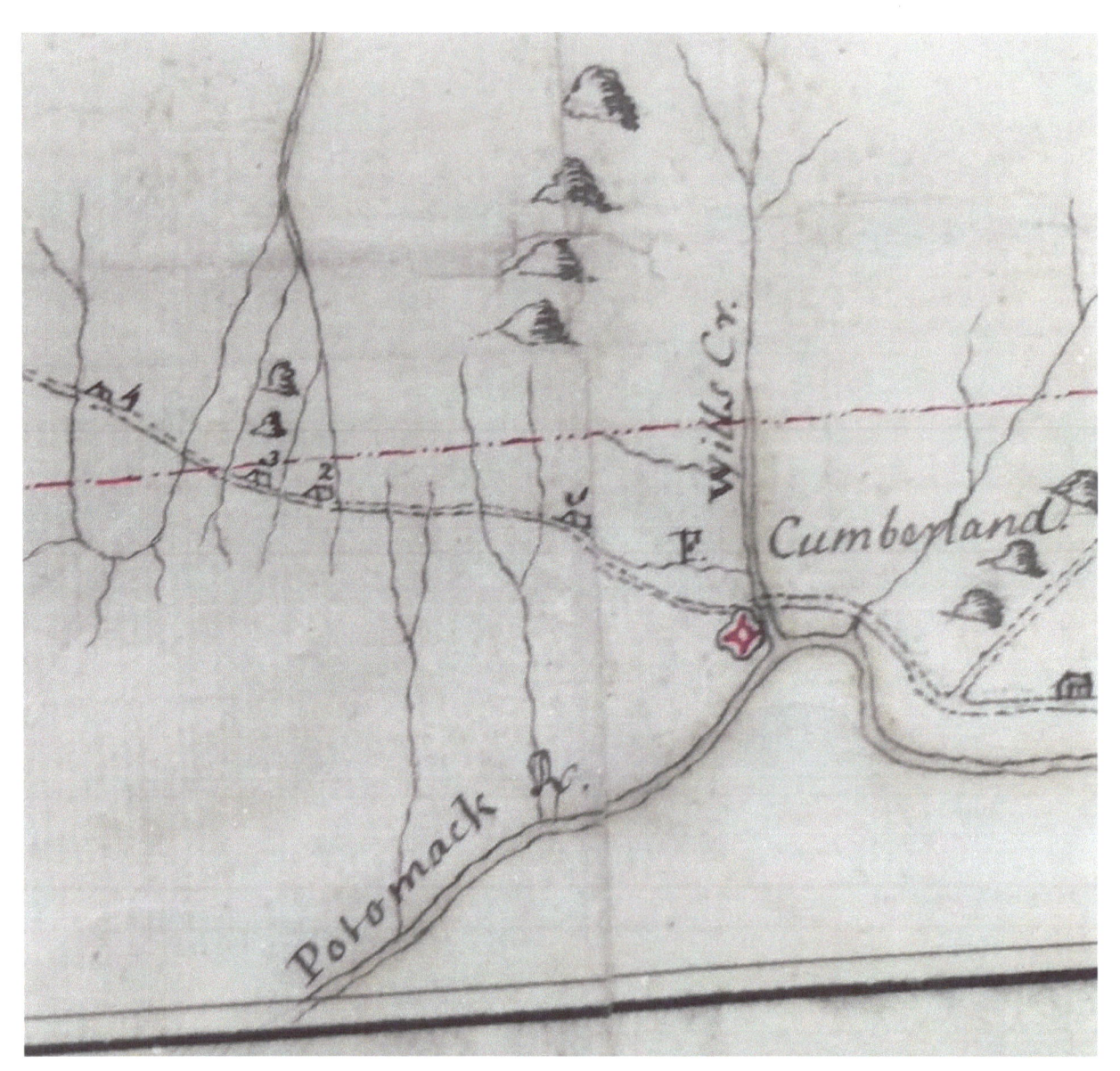

Figure 24 — This is from a map that is titled "**Military Sketch from Philadelphia to Fort Du Quesne**" and bears a July 12, 1758 date. The map covers a large portion of Pennsylvania, and shows a great many waterways, roads, and paths. The map erroneously illustrates the Georges Creek camp (camp no. 2) within the watershed of the Youghiogheny River, and locates the third and fourth camps where Gist locates the fourth and fifth camps. This portion of the map seems obviously to be based on the Gist map of Figure 21, yet makes these significant mistakes regarding the camp locations. This map is included to show just how wrong large area maps can be when it comes to details that the author is unfamiliar with. For whatever reason, this map shows the road swinging to the northwest along the head portion of Braddock Run before reaching Georges Creek. As a result, this map provides no support for the idea that Braddock's road followed Hoffman Hollow.

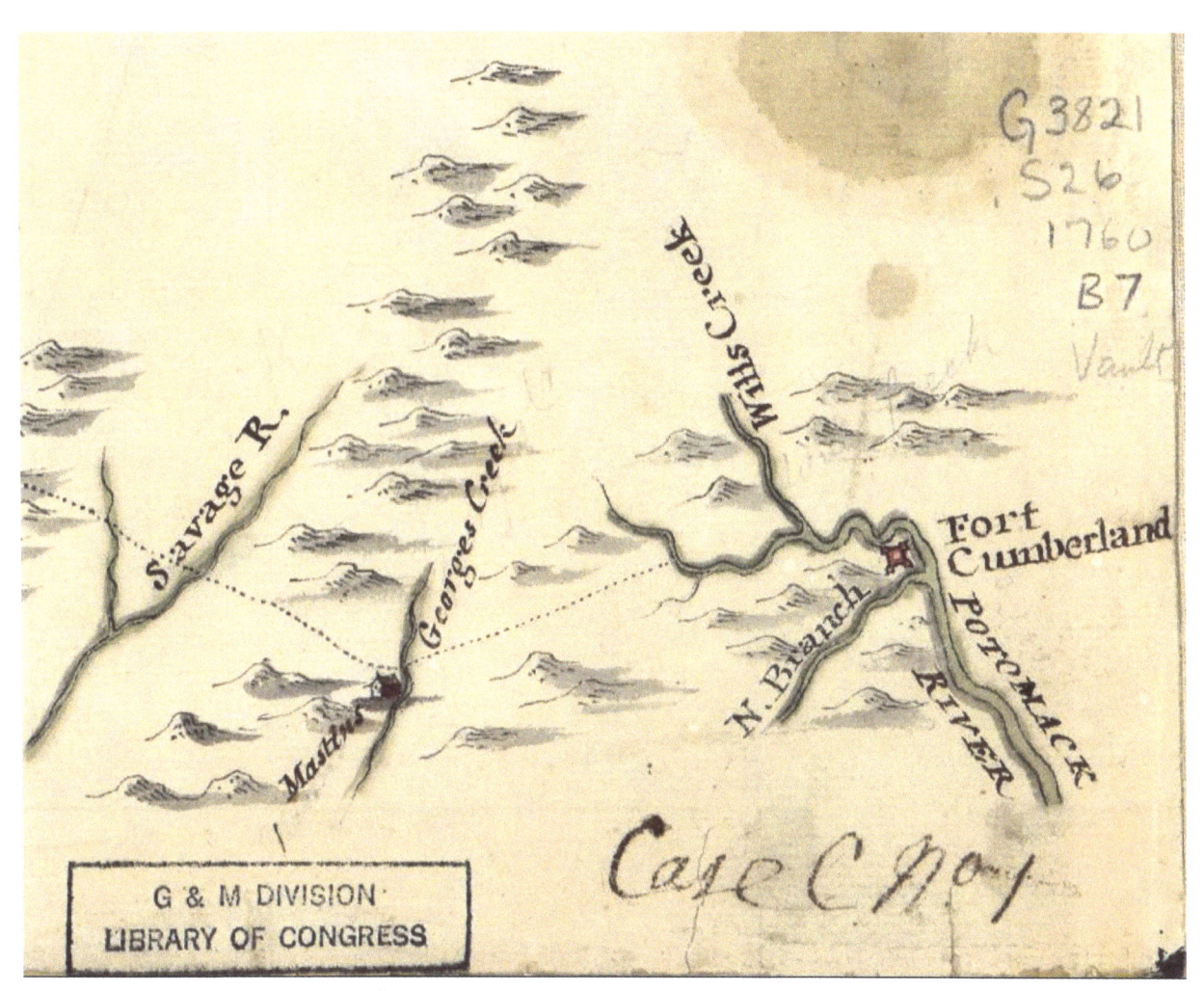

Figure 25 — This is a circa 1759/60 map that includes Braddock's road and Martin's plantation (Library of Congress Call No. G3821.S26 1760 .B7). It clearly illustrates Martin's plantation as being located west of Georges Creek, and clearly illustrates the route of Braddock's road as traveling west-southwest between Porter Run and Martin's plantation. Look at the excellent depiction of Braddock Run on this map. If you were using this map to travel to Martin's plantation, you would know to follow Braddock Run southwest to its westerly turn at Allegany Grove, then follow it through the slightly winding valley between Dans Mountain and Piney Mountain (note the accurate depiction of the curving waterway), and then you would know to turn right at Clarysville to follow the main branch (now known as Porter Run) toward the village of Eckhart Mines. You would also know that the road strikes off from Porter Run to reach Martin's plantation. To fully appreciate how accurately this map depicts Braddock Run, compare it to a LIDAR map.

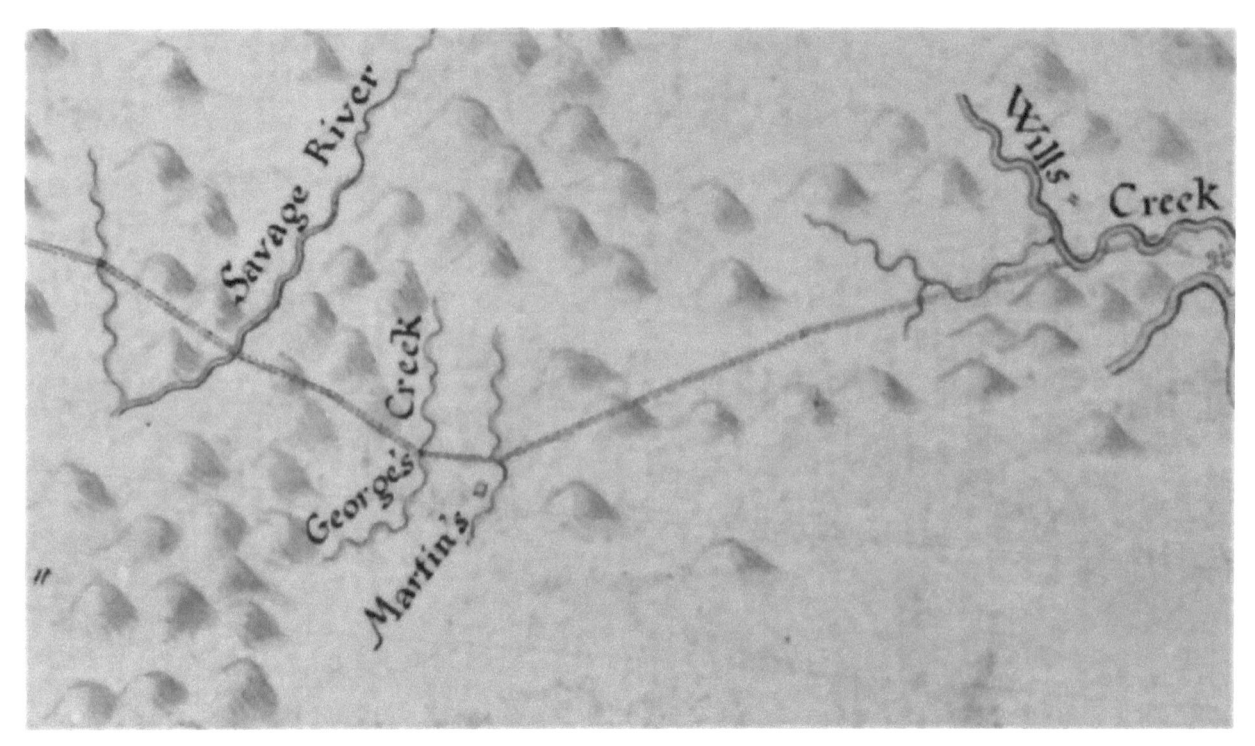

Figure 26 — This is from one of three similar maps at the British Archives. I refer to this map as *"the red Fort Cumberland map"* because both the icon of the fort and the words "Fort Cumberland" are red. The lower margin of this map includes the statement *"Doen by Elias Meyer Engineer. L.ᵗ in the 60ᵗʰ Regᵗ."* This map incorporates plans of Fort Presu'Isle, Fort Le Beuf, Fort Venango, and Fort Pitt. On this map, Martin's residence is located west of the eastern head fork of Georges Creek.

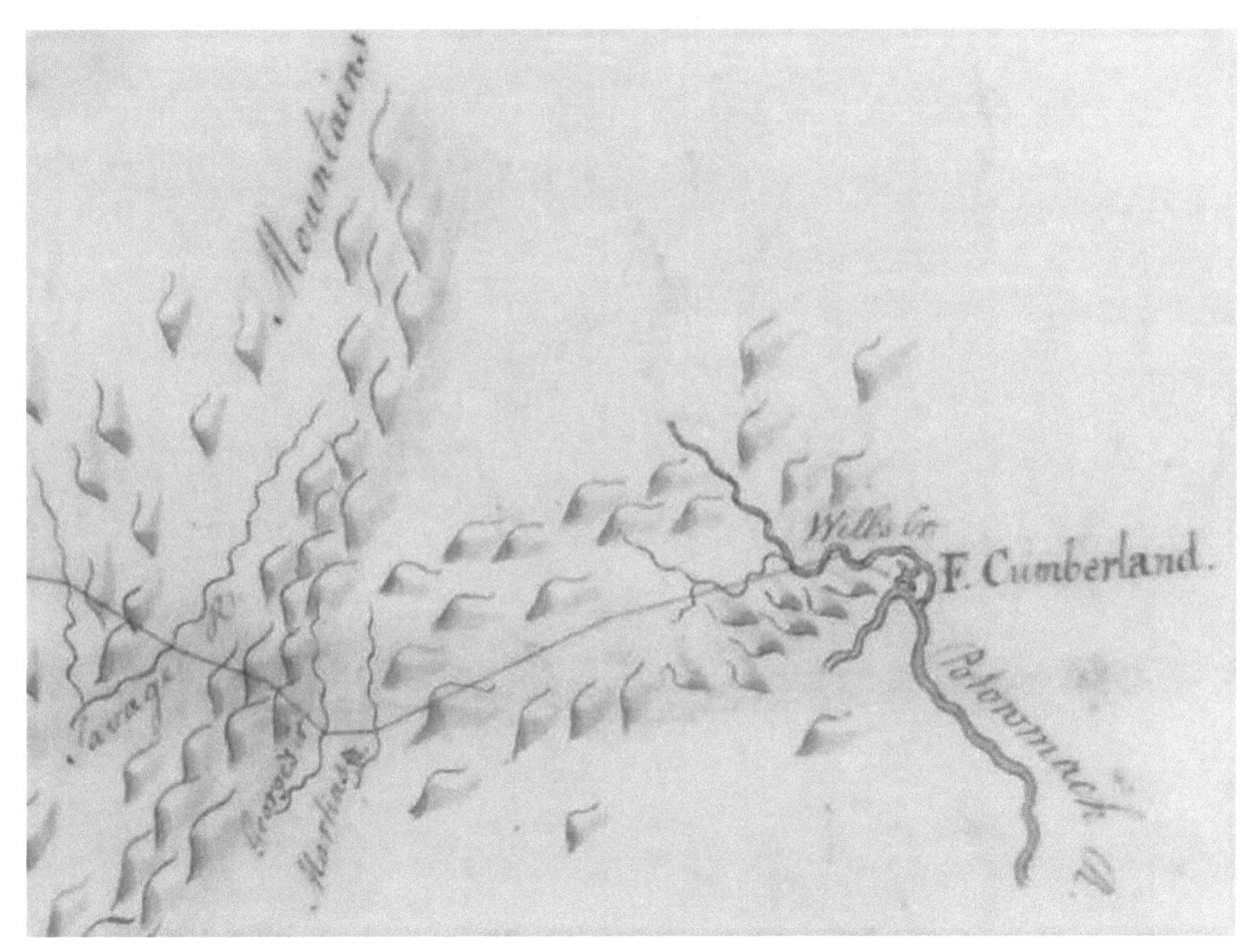

Figure 27 — This is from one of three similar maps at the British Archives. I refer to this map as *"the black Fort Cumberland map"* because the icon of the fort is black. This version of the map bears conspicous red broad arrow stamps. As with the other variations of this map, Martin's residence is located west of the eastern head fork of Georges Creek.

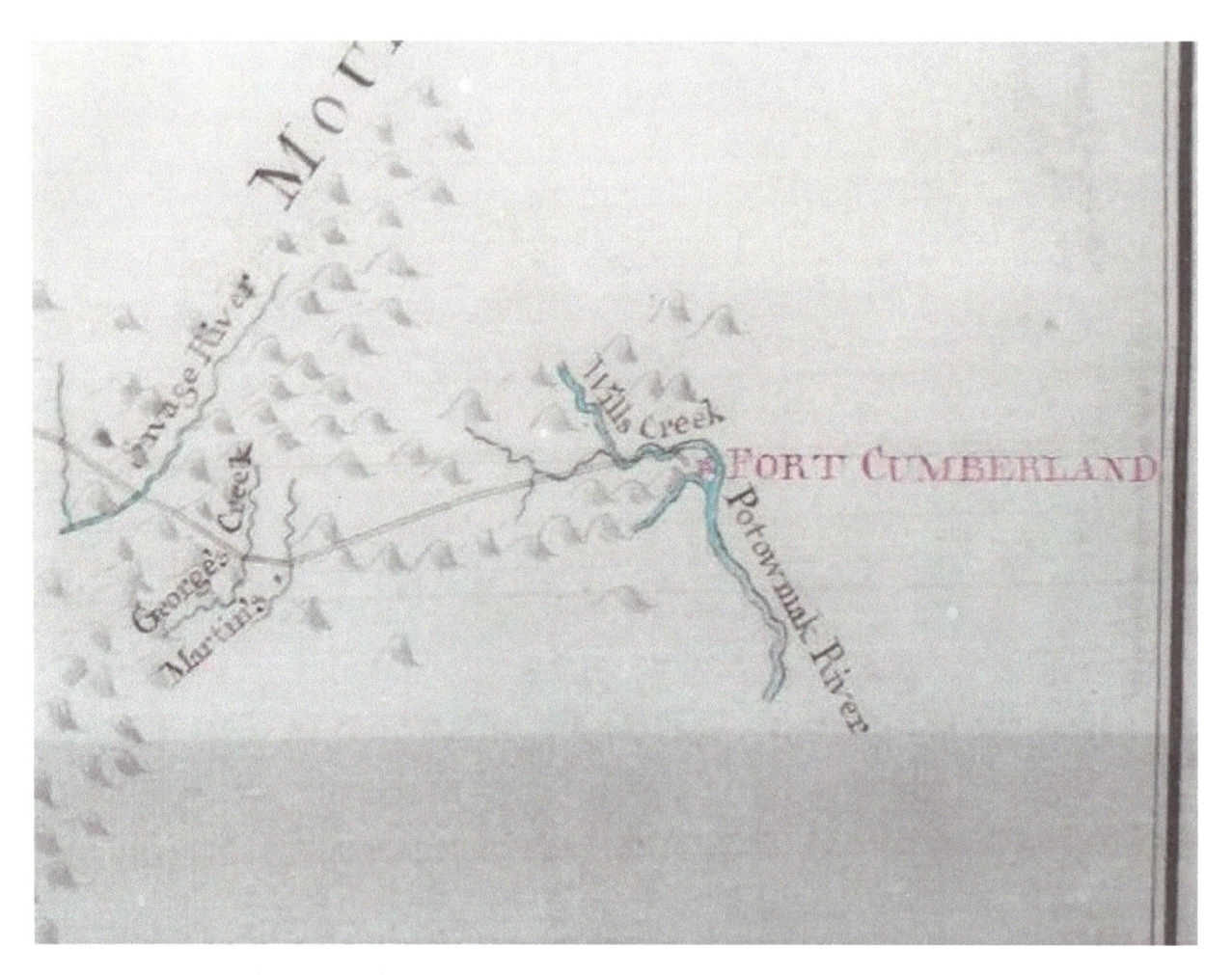

Figure 28 — This is from one of three similar maps at the British Archives. I refer to this map as *"the red-green Fort Cumberland map"* because the icon of the fort and the words *"Fort Cumberland"* are red, and some of the waterways are blue-green. As with the other variations of this map, Martin's residence is located west of the eastern head fork of Georges Creek.

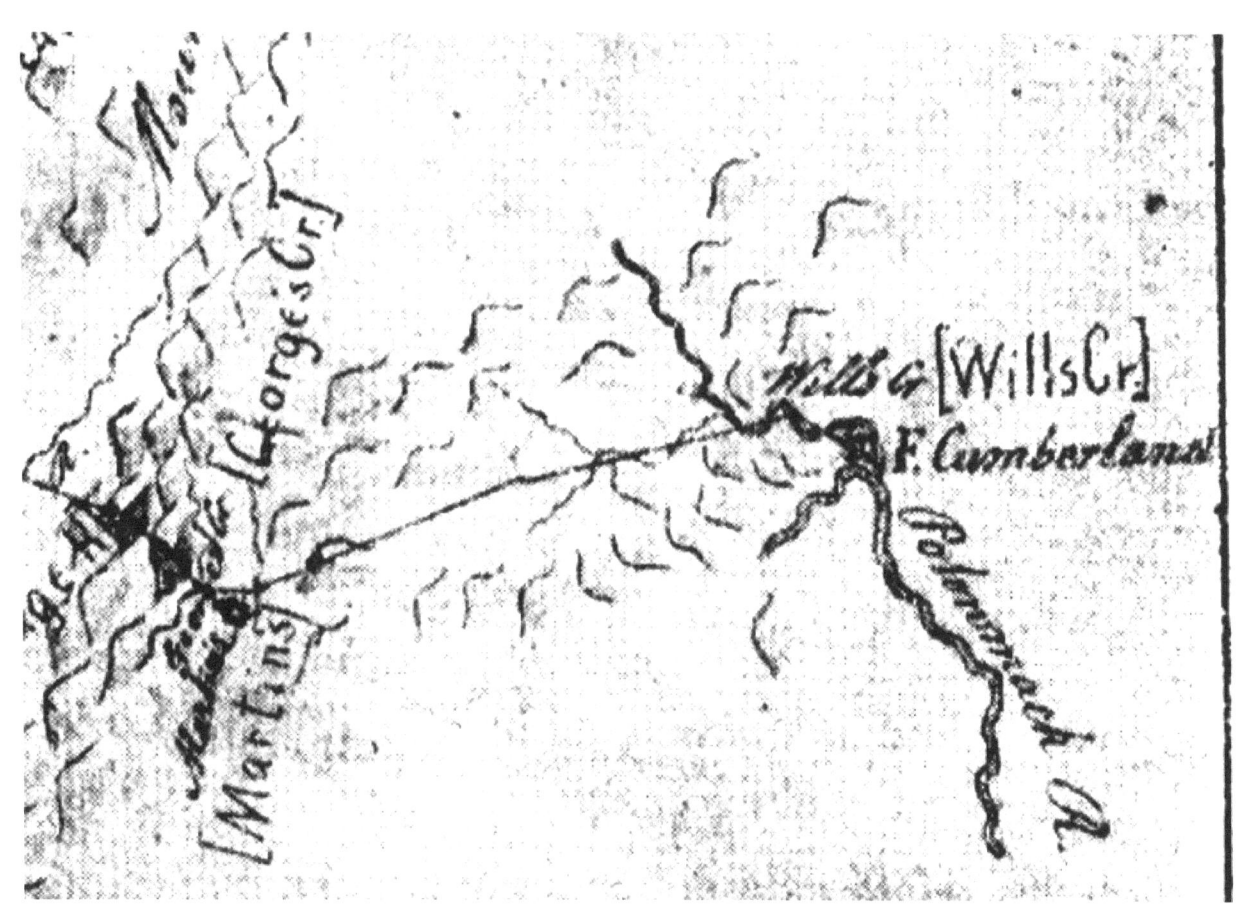

Figure 29 — This is from a map that Hulbert describes as Shippen's November, 1759 "**Draught of The Monongahela & Youghiogany Rivers**". This map also illustrates Martin's plantation as being located west of Georges Creek.

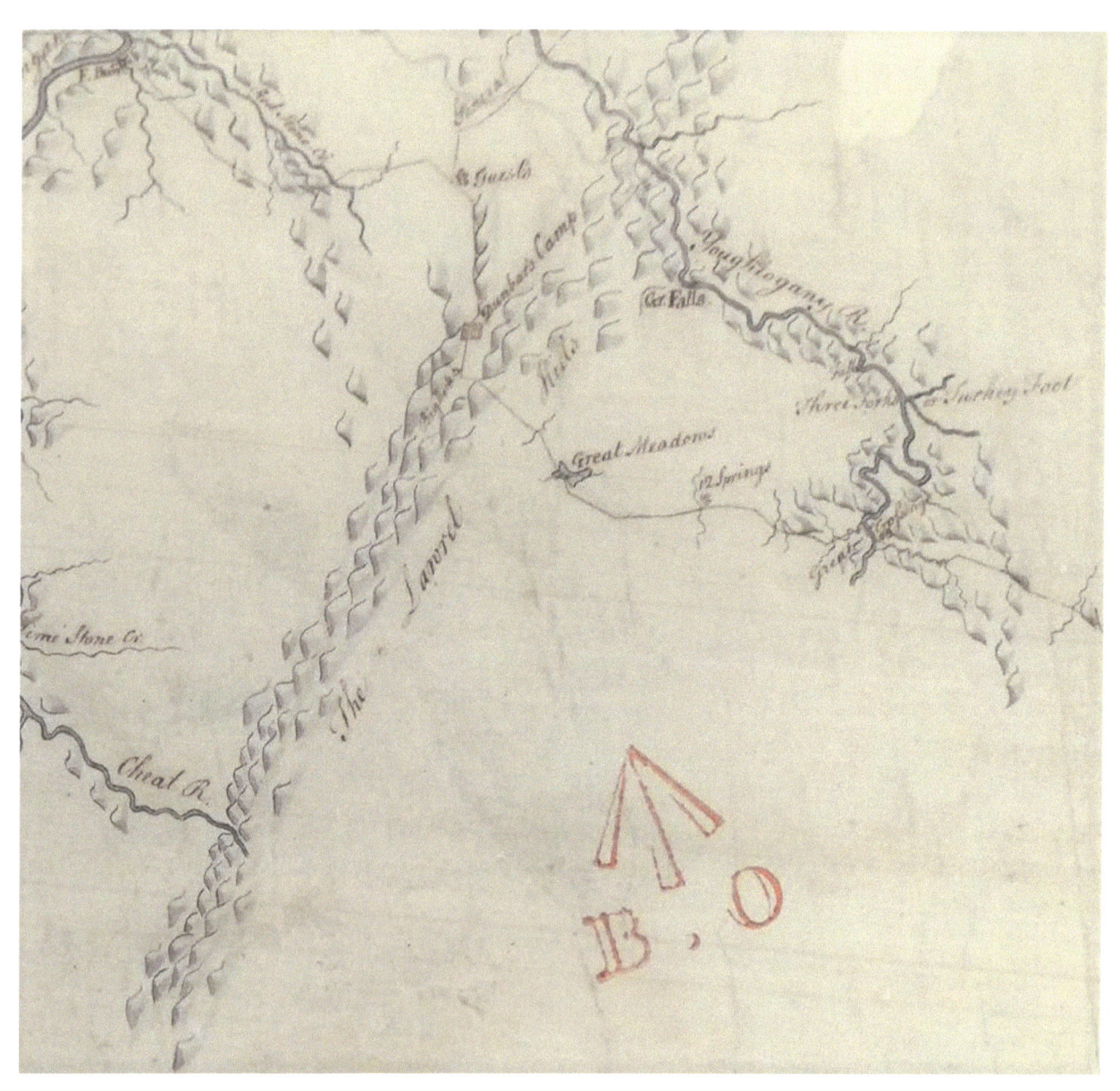

Figure 30 — This is a view of more of *"the black Fort Cumberland map"* that is included as Figure 27. It is included for comparison with the Hulbert map of Figure 31. Compare the roads depicted in the vicinity of Gist's (*"Guest's"*) plantation.

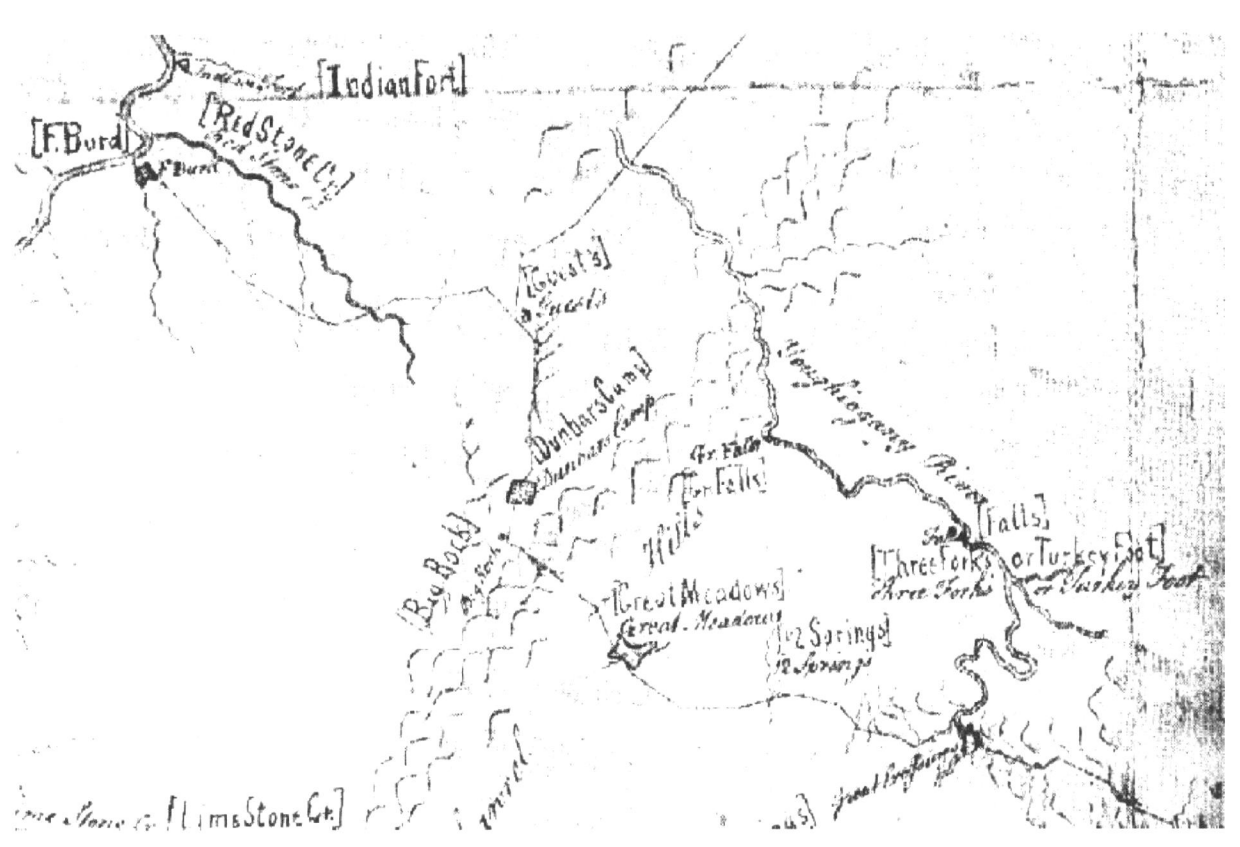

Figure 31 — This is a view of more of the Hulbert map that is included as Figure 29. It is included for comparison with the view of *"the black Fort Cumberland map"* that is included as Figure 30. Compare the roads depicted in the vicinity of Gist's (*"Guest's"*) plantation. Hulbert describes this as Shippen's November, 1759 **"Draught of The Monongahela & Youghiogany Rivers"**. The identification of Fort Burd on this map dates it to sometime after September 30, 1759.[99]

---

[99] Burd wrote a letter to Stanwix from the *"Camp at the mouth of Nemoraling's Creek, on the Monongahela, about one mile above the mouth of Redstone Creek, Sept. 30th, 1759."* On the same day, Bouquet wrote a letter to Burd from Bedford that includes the statement, *"I am glad you could find such a pretty situation for your Post. Give it a shorter name than the wild one of the Creek."* A letter Bouquet wrote from Pittsburgh on October 24, 1759 references *"Burd's Fort"*.

11. Martin's plantation

Martin's plantation had pasture land

As quoted previously in a footnote, an entry in Braddock's orderly book[100] for May 15, 1755, written from Fort Cumberland prior to the expedition, includes the statement:

One subaltern, one serg[t] 1 corpl and 30 cent'l to march this evening to Mr. Martin's where the troop of Light Horse graze, the men to take tents with them and provisions for three days, the officer to receive his orders from Captain Stuart of the Light Horse; this guard to be relievd every 3d Day.

This order indicates that Martin's plantation had pasture.

General Braddock camped at Martin's during the expedition

On June 15, 1755, Elizabeth Martin wrote a letter to her brother stating that General Braddock, along with his staff, *"camped here last night"* and while there, had a discussion with a member of the household, providing the news that Abram Martin was taking his command on Braddock's expedition.[101]

The Martin plantation was raided overnight

There is one thing in Elizabeth Martin's letter that must be considered when theorizing that the camp was located between the head forks of Georges Creek. The letter indicates that during the night of June 14, 1755, *"last night"*, the outbuildings and barns on the Martin plantation were burned, and all of their horses and fowl were taken. Unless Braddock's forces committed these acts, the letter suggests that the farmstead[102] itself was not occupied by the main part of Braddock's forces. Still, if we are looking for Braddock's second camp, this letter seems to indicate that the general himself camped at Martin's plantation. One simple explanation for the failure to protect Martin's barns and outbuildings is the possibility that Braddock's forces were massed on and near the road and in the fields, and the possibility that the farmstead was not located directly on the road — for example, it may have been located near one of the springs that are described below.

Some may wish to use the letter to suggest that Braddock's forces weren't there to protect the outbuildings because they were camped at the consensus camp location on the east side of Georges Creek. This would be inconsistent with the idea expressed by some that as an early settler, Martin's plantation would have been located on the arguably better ground to be found on the east side of Georges Creek. Turning this line of reasoning on its head, if despite all the map-based evidence, Martin's plantation was actually located on the east side of Georges Creek, then the thinness of defense at Martin's plantation on the night of June 14, 1755 would be a modest point in favor of the main encampment being located on the west side of Georges Creek. This isn't as far-fetched

---

[100] **"History of Cumberland"**, Lowdermilk, 1878.
[101] For the complete text of this letter, see the 1939 book **"Genealogy of the Martin, Marshall & Edwards Families Who Settled in Virginia, and of the Quin Family of Mississippi"**.
[102] I.e., the house, barns, and other outbuildings.

as it sounds, because Braddock's camps were huge affairs,[103] and the maps may simply indicate where a significant portion of Braddock's forces camped. No evidence that I am aware of precludes the camp from straddling both sides of Georges Creek — but I am not personally aware of any 1700s military equipment being found at the location of the consensus campsite.

Orme's account describes the location of the second camp relative to Savage Mountain

Orme's account of Braddock's expedition[104] is included in Winthrop Sargent's 1855 book "**The History of an Expedition against fort Du Quesne, in 1755…**" Page 333 includes the statement:

> *It required two days to new load the waggons, and put everything in order, which being settled we marched on the 13th to Martin's plantation, being about five miles from Spendelow Camp. The first brigade got to their ground that night, but the second could not get up before the next day at eleven of the clock, the road being excessively mountainous and rocky. This obliged the General to halt one day for the refreshment of the men and horses.*

One consideration for locating the second camp at Martin's plantation would have been pasture. The horses and livestock that accompanied the expedition would have been grazing in Martin's fields, and may have consumed some of any stored forage Martin had on hand. Given these opportunities, the expedition would be unlikely to feed the animals from any forage carried by the wagons.

Another consideration for locating the second camp would have been plentiful water for the horses and livestock — something springs alone would be unlikely to have the capacity to supply. If the main part of the camp was located between the head forks of Georges creek (as the maps indicate), the animals would have had a chance to drink from Georges Creek on the way into camp, which ever day they arrived, and to get another drink from Sand Spring Run on the way out of camp on the 15th. Any animals that were in camp more than one night would have needed occasional access to one of the streams.

Lacock's projected second campsite, just east of Georges Creek, would be superior to my hypothetical camp location from the standpoint of ready access to water, because it is bounded on three sides by Georges Creek and a small northerly flowing tributary. It would, however, be inferior from a tactical standpoint, being located on lower ground.

---

[103] Orme's eyewitness description of Spendelow Camp informs us of the immense size of Braddock's camps, stating, *"We were now encamped according to the plan approved of by the Council of War. When the carriages were closed up, leaving proper intervals of communications, the extent of the Camp, from the front to the rear guard, was less than half a mile."*

[104] On September 5, 1755, Orme wrote a letter to General Shirley stating, *"Captain Orme is going to England, and will put the affair of the western campaign in a true light, and greatly different from what it has been represented to be; and you know his situation and abilities gave him great opportunities of knowing everything that passed in the army or in the colony, relative to military matters, and I am sure he will be of great use to the Ministry in the measures that may be concerted for the future safety and defence of these provinces."* (Pages 283-284, **"The History of an Expedition against fort Du Quesne, in 1755…"**)

Regarding the second camp, Orme also states:

June 15th. The line began to move from this place at five of the clock; it was twelve before all the carriages had got upon a hill which is about a quarter of a mile from the front of the Camp, and it was found necessary to make one-half of the men ground their arms and assist the carriages while the others remained advantageously posted for their security.

We this day passed the Aligany Mountain, which is a rocky ascent of more than two miles, in many places extremely steep; its descent is very rugged and almost perpendicular; in passing which we intirely demolished three waggons and shattered several. At the bottom of the mountain runs Savage river, which, when we passed was an insignificant stream; but the Indians assured us that in the winter it is very deep, broad and rapid. This is the last water that empties itself into the Potomack.

The first Brigade encamped about three miles to the westward of this river. Near this place was another steep ascent, which the waggons were six hours in passing.

In this day's march, though all possible care was taken, the line was sometimes extended to a length of four or five miles.

Engineer Harry Gordon, who was with an advance engineering party of 600 men, recorded the following in his journal on May 31, 1755, "Little Meadows – 10 Miles – A great deal of cutting, digging and bridging and a great deal of blowing[105] – 4 miles up and down the ridge very rough and steep, the rest for about 5 miles tolerable, 1 mile rough and a hard pinch – camp inclosed with an abates,[106] dry, fine feeding, good water scarce – 3 days."

The previously presented maps indicate that the second camp was located between the head forks of Georges Creek. The western fork is known as Sand Spring Run, which can be thought of as defining the start of Savage Mountain. Obviously, Savage Mountain is Gordon's four-mile-wide ridge and Orme's *"hill which is about a quarter of a mile from the front of the Camp."* There is no other hill near any projected location of the second camp that would require seven hours to ascend. When viewed in the context of the early maps, Orme's June 15, 1755 journal entry suggests that the western edge of the second camp (at Martin's plantation) was located about 440 yards (1/4 mile) east of Sand Spring Run. If the traditional route of Braddock's road through Frostburg is reasonably accurate (for example, as shown on Figure 12), this interpretation puts the western edge of the camp at or near the entrance to Frostburg State University on present-day Braddock Road, at approximately latitude 39.648306°, longitude -78.932711°.

To be fair, the eastern slope of Savage Mountain could also be considered to start at the eastern fork of Georges Creek. This interpretation of Orme's *"hill which is about a quarter of a mile from the front of the Camp"* would be harmonious with Lacock's projected location of the second camp, but it would not be harmonious with the various contemporaneous maps that locate the second camp and Martin's plantation between the head forks of Georges Creek. One interesting factor is

---

[105] This is a reference to blasting rocks with gunpowder.
[106] Abbatis.

that Orme reports that the first and second brigades got into camp on different days. Based on his report, one might suspect that the first brigade was camped farther west than the second brigade.

A cannonball was found at the camp location theorized by this book

Robert Kenney found a cannonball and other artifacts near the entrance to Frostburg State University.[107] This is not definitive proof of the location of the second camp, because the general route was used by various other eighteenth century military parties. It is, however, certainly harmonious with the theory that the camp was located in that area. As stated previously, I am not aware of any similar evidence found on the consensus campsite location, east of Georges Creek.

The last muzzle loading artillery to move westward from Fort Cumberland may have occurred in 1780. That year, Captain Isaac Craig delivered stores and a detachment of Procter's artillery from Carlisle to Fort Pitt via Fort Cumberland. A memorandum of his march lists various stops west of Fort Cumberland as follows: June 8, Fort Cumberland; June 9, Halls; June 10, Tittle's, June 11, Tomlinson's; June 12 & 13, Bear Camp; June 14, Rice's; June 15, Big Meadows.[108] If the cannonball that Robert Kenney found happed to be from this expedition, it would suggest that the traditional route of Braddock's road through Frostburg already existed in 1780.

Water sources on the projected site of the second camp

A plat of Beall's First Addition to Frostburg is included as Figure 32.[109] The plat identifies the location of two public springs, including one on Spring Street and one on Alley 33 between Center and Bowery streets.[110] These springs may help to identify the possible locations of Abram Martin's residence — assuming that the location of Martin's residence that is shown on Figure 25 and Figure 31 is accurate.

It seems likely that there was also a spring somewhere on the flanks of Welsh Hill, which is located at latitude 39.646851°, longitude -78.931690°.[111] This potential spring and the two verified springs are probably not enough to water all the animals — a stream would probably be required for that — but it represents a lot more water than men at Bushy Run had[112] — if the springs were not dried up as a result of the severe drought. With two or three possible springs on defensible high ground, and two streams located nearby to water the animals while encamped and when entering and leaving camp, the projected site of the second camp on the west side of Georges Creek does not seem to be the worst place that was ever chosen to resist a potential enemy attack.

---

[107] The artifact finds were reported by Dave Williams. Unfortunately, we do not know the size of the cannonball.

[108] Craig's memorandum is included in Volume 2 of the 1880 book "**Pennsylvania in the War of the Revolution, Battalions and Line...**"

[109] This map was identified by Julia Jackson.

[110] Jennifer Simon-Likens reports that there is a natural spring on Spring Street that runs through her property.

[111] The location of the local landmark known as Welsh Hill was identified by Chad Paul.

[112] A contemporaneous account of the 1763 battle of Bushy Run, written by John Ormsby, describes the difficulty of fighting without water, stating, *"The English troops were in a wretched situation, as the Indians very artfully secured all the springs of water in the neighborhood. Thus they (the English) fought all day without water, except what they sucked out of the tracks of beasts, as happily a small rain fell."*

I concede that the severe drought may have even dried up the small, spring-fed head forks of Georges Creek. This is really immaterial to the discussion of the camp location, however, because it would have deprived Lacock's projected campsite of readily available water from the head forks as well.

Speculation aside, Engineer Harry Gordon recorded the following in his journal on May 30, 1755, *"to Martin's – 5 miles – A great deal of cutting, digging and bridging – One mile level but swampy, 2 ½ miles very rough and steep, the rest tolerable but here and there swampy – camp open, dry, very good feeding, fine water – 1 day."* There seems to have been plenty of water for the 600-man advance party Gordon was with. The reference to feeding probably concerns feeding the animals that were with the party. This and the reference to the openness of the camp suggest they were literally at Martin's plantation, rather than merely nearby, and grazing their animals in his fields.

Figure 32 — This is a portion of a plat of Beall's First Addition to Frostburg (plat book 1, page 136). It shows the location of two public springs. One is marked with an X, and the other is marked *"Public Spring Lot"*.

12. More recent documents

A 1793 document locates Braddock's road on the Mountain tract

A law recorded in the 1793 "**Laws of Maryland**" that is titled *"An Act to establish the road from the Turkey Foot Road towards Braddock's road as a public road, and for other purposes therein mentioned"* states:

> WHEREAS Sundry inhabitants of Allegany county, by their petition to this general assembly have set forth, that there hath been a road from the Turkey Foot road, above the fork of Jenning's Run,[113] leading up the said run by Oswalt's saw-mill[114] to the foot of Mount-Pleasant,[115] and from thence until it intersects Bradock's road at a tract of land called The Mountain, and that, it never having been made a public road by law, they are deprived of the benefit and utility of the same...

This law is reasonable evidence that the road that was known as Braddock's road in 1793 crossed the Mountain tract that is illustrated on the 1953 map of Frostburg (Figure 12). This helps to corroborate the traditional route of Braddock's road that is shown on the 1953 map.

The 1794 Dennis Griffith map

The 1794 Dennis Griffith map[116] (Figure 33) was made at a time when maps were becoming slightly less schematic, and wagons were creating the sunken roads we study today. The curved route between Cumberland and Gwynn's *("Quinn's")* tavern is a good match to the route depicted by individuals who research Braddock road, as is the route between Gwynn's and Tittles, if this Tittle's residence was located at or near Clarysville. The map shows many intricate twists and turns in the southerly path to Westernport along the west side of Georges Creek, and shows a radical turn of the road that ran between Tomlinson's and Simpkin's *("Simkin's")* taverns. With this level of detail, one has to wonder why Lacock's radial turn at the top of Hoffman Hollow is missing, and why the road is schematically illustrated as running west-northwest between Tittle's and the present-day site of Frostburg.[117] That schematic northward leaning line does not necessarily represent Braddock's original route. Still, it suggests that the most popular though-route may have been going up through the site of the present-day village of Eckhart Mines in 1794. In any case, the schematic line certainly provides no support for Temple's assumption that early travelers would in general follow Braddock's alleged trace up Hoffman Hollow. If, as Temple

---

[113] This is a reference to the site of present-day Barrelville, Maryland, where the North Branch of Jennings Run joins the branch flowing down from the village of Mount Savage. The *phrase "above the fork of Jenning's Run"* means uphill (i.e., upstream) from the North Branch of Jennings Run.

[114] Oswalt's saw-mill was probably the predecessor to Johnathan Arnold's grist mill, on the north side of Maryland Route 36, across from Woodcock Hollow Road. See analysis in the book "**In Search of the Turkey Foot Road**", fourth edition, Dietle & McKenzie.

[115] The tract of land known as *"Mount Pleasant"* was located between the sites of the present-day towns of Frostburg and Mount Savage. It encompassed the mountain that lies on the west side of the portion of Jennings Run that runs from Frostburg to Mount Savage.

[116] The 1794 Griffith map of the state of Maryland was brought to my attention by the late Steve Colby.

[117] The 1791 map of Pennsylvania by Adlum and Wallis also shows Braddock's road passing through the head forks of Georges Creek, i.e., the site of present-day Frostburg.

assumed, *"early travelers would in general follow that trace rather than cut a new way through the forest"*, then the Griffith map suggests they were following that trace up along Porter Run.

One argument I've encountered regarding the location of Martin's plantation is the perfectly reasonable observation that the ground east of the eastern head fork of Georges Creek is fairly level, and more desirable as farmland, compared to the ground west of Spring Street. As one who has studied the early history of far western Maryland, I can certainly attest that the earliest settlers did usually locate on the best available ground.

The 1794 Griffith map shows that the path to Westernport passed through the present-day site of Frostburg and came from Pennsylvania. It isn't difficult to conclude, with a high degree of confidence, that this is the road mentioned in the previously quoted 1793 Maryland law. John Mitchell's 1755 map (Figure 34), titled "**A map of the British and French dominions in North America**", apparently shows this path connecting with Raystown (now Bedford, Pennsylvania). These maps suggest that Martin's plantation was located at an intersection of two traders paths; one from Raystown and one from Fort Cumberland and the Ohio Company storehouse in Ridgeley. This helps to explain why Martin's plantation was located between the head forks of Georges Creek instead of on the arguably better ground just east of the eastern fork. By locating at the intersection, Martin presumably would have been able to generate income by selling forage to feed the packhorse trains of traders.

The mid-1800s Frostburg Coal Company map

The earliest modern-era map that I am aware of that purports to show Braddock's route through Frostburg is the mid-1800s "**Map of the Frostburg Coal Company's Lands.**" This map[118] (Figure 35) has utility because it shows the traditional route of Braddock's road relative to the northern tip of the Walnutt Levill survey. Although this map is somewhat schematic, it seems to illustrate Braddock's road as being located a little closer to the northern tip of Walnutt Levill, compared to the 1953 map of Figure 12. This difference may help to explain why the old milestone known as Braddock's stone (Figure 36) is located north of the illustrated route on the 1953 map. It was not uncommon for early roads to become displaced from their original route over time, while retaining the original name. I do not know, however, if this milestone was restored to its original location when it was repaired and covered with a pagoda in 1890.[119]

In Frostburg, Spring Street is located on relatively level elevated ground, near a relatively steep hillside that drops down to Georges Creek. Figure 37 is a survey of the Taylor lot on Spring Street that shows the traditional route of Braddock's road climbing the hillside, and the old sunken road

---

[118] The map was provided by David Williams.

[119] An article in an 1890 issue of the "**Civilian**" newspaper states, *"Some Frostburg Michael Angelo has hacked it in two with intent to use it for some base and ignoble purpose and in any event we are glad to see the old landmark covered with a Pagoda, though the price paid for it, $275.84, would appear to show that the Frostburg lumbermen, carpenters, painters and tinkers apparently knew a good thing upon sight, even if the village Michael Angelo didn't."* (Quoted from a published speech that was given by Robert L. Bantz at the dedication of the new Braddock's stone pavilion on September 13, 2012.) An older document at the Frostburg museum reports that the milestone was standing near the Pullen School at the time the document was written, but had formerly been located on the lot of Charles Conrad.

is still there to this day. Terrain, the Gist maps, the *"Gordon map"*, and the *"Orme map"*, the circa-1759/60 manuscript map, and the desirability of a defensible camp location on high ground with natural springs, suggest that Martin's plantation and Braddock's second camp may have been located on the high ground west of the hillside.

In his 1912 book, Lacock states the old milestone was then located about 350 feet north of Braddock Park. When considered in the light of Orme's *"quarter of a mile from the front of the Camp"* statement, Braddock Park seems to have been located within the bounds of Braddock's second encampment. The image of Braddock Park from the Braddock Road postcard series (Figure 38) shows that the park was situated on reasonable ground for a campsite.

On Figure 35, there is a road running north from Meshach Frost's residence along the traditional route of Braddock's road, and a dot near Sand Spring Run seems to be the *"C. & S. Musselman, May 30th, 1806"* springhouse that Lacock described. The road running north from Frost's is mentioned by an August 19, 1819 road survey (Figure 39) that references Christian Musselman's tavern as being located on Braddock's road. This survey indicates that the traditional route of Braddock's road through Frostburg was already known as Braddock's road in 1819.

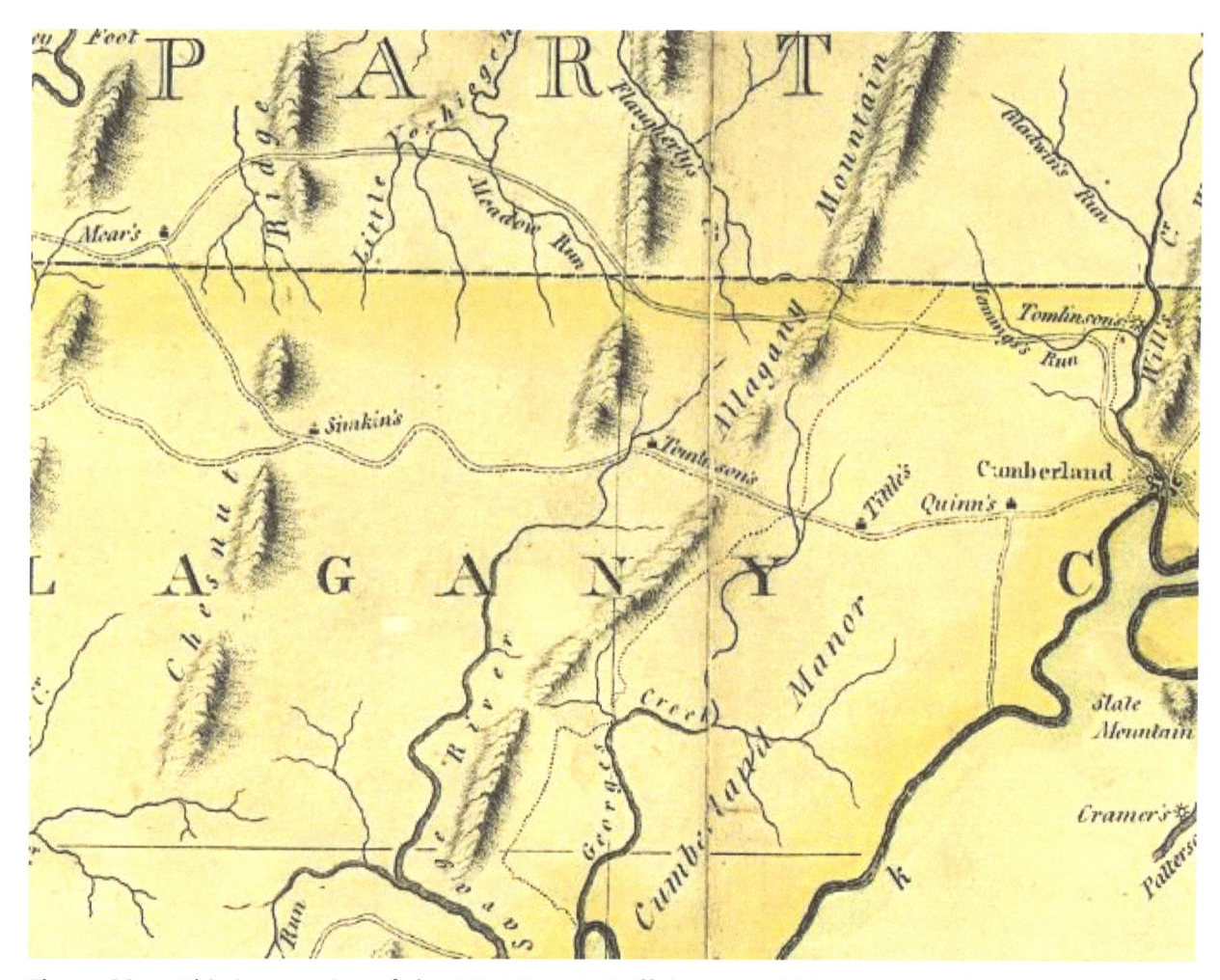

Figure 33 — This is a portion of the 1794 Dennis Griffith map, which was printed in 1795 (Library of Congress Call No. G3840 1794 .G72). It illustrates the various twists and turns of a north-northeasterly path from Westernport that passed through the head forks of Georges Creek. Just east of Simkin's tavern, it also illustrates a radical bend in the then-existing version of Braddock's road — and yet it does not illustrate Lacock's radial northerly turn toward the site of present-day Frostburg.

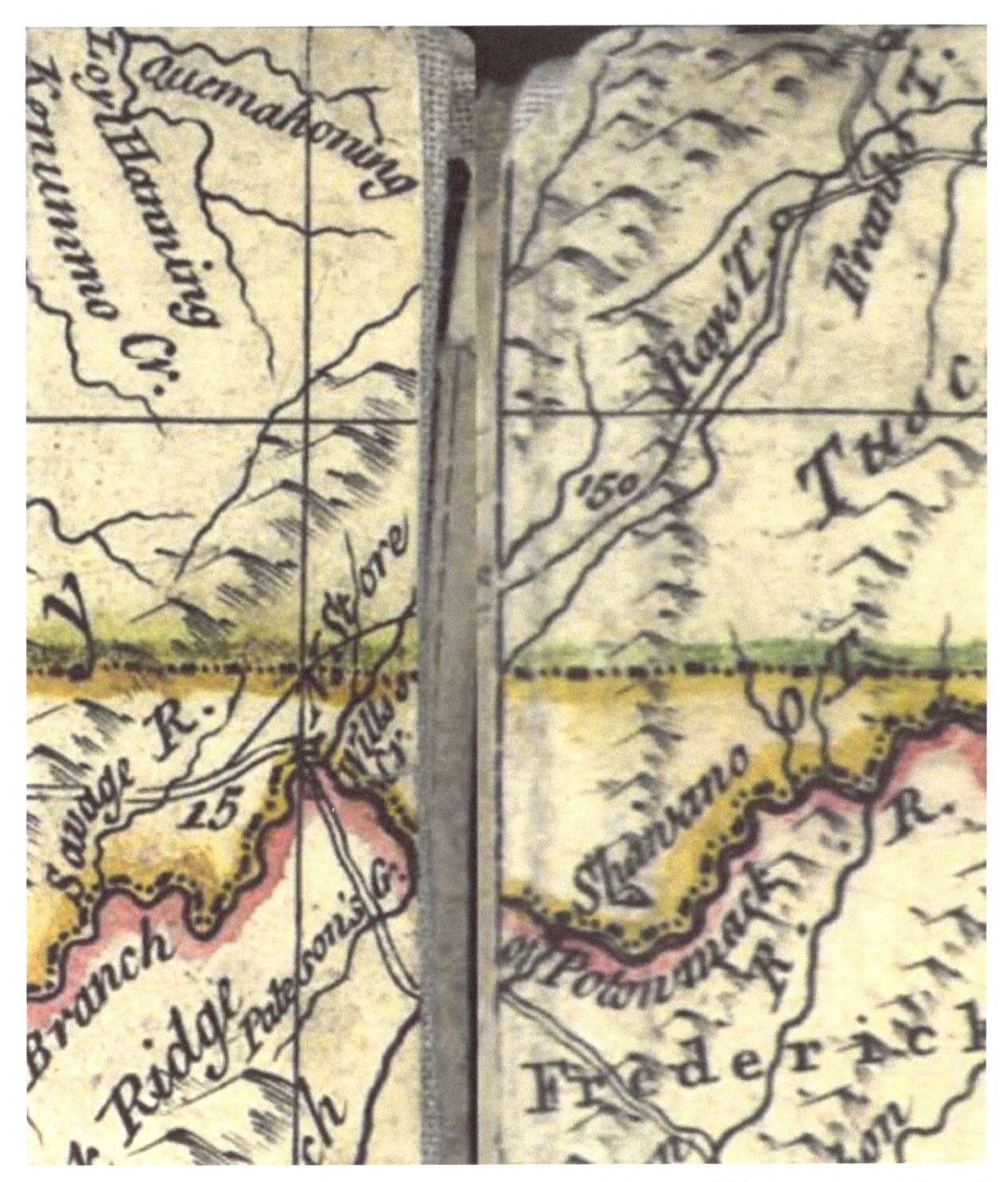

Figure 34 — This is a portion of the February 13, 1755 Mitchell map, which shows the path from the present-day site of Frostburg extending to Raystown (Library of Congress Call No. G3300 1755 .M53). This path provides a plausible theoretical reason for Martin's plantation to be located within the head forks of Georges Creek: To sell forage to traders traveling to and from Wills Creek and Raystown.

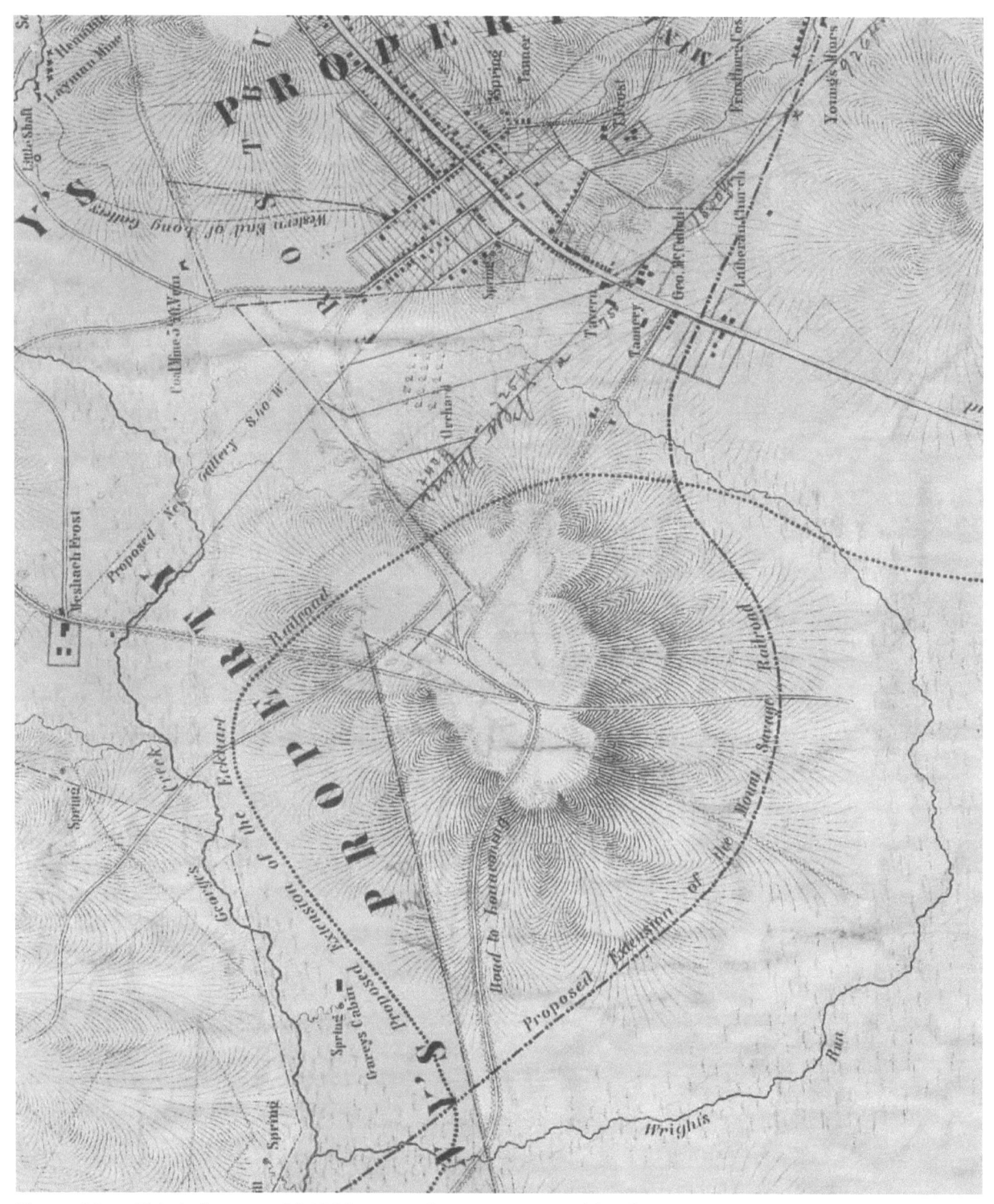

Figure 35 — This is from a mid-1800s map of property owned by the Frostburg Coal Company. Meshack Frost's home is illustrated as being on the traditional route of Braddock's road. The small black rectangle between the Frost residence and the creek may represent the 1806 Musselman springhouse Lacock described. The spring that is located near Taylor Street and the bend in the National Pike is one of the fountainheads of the eastern head fork of Georges Creek.

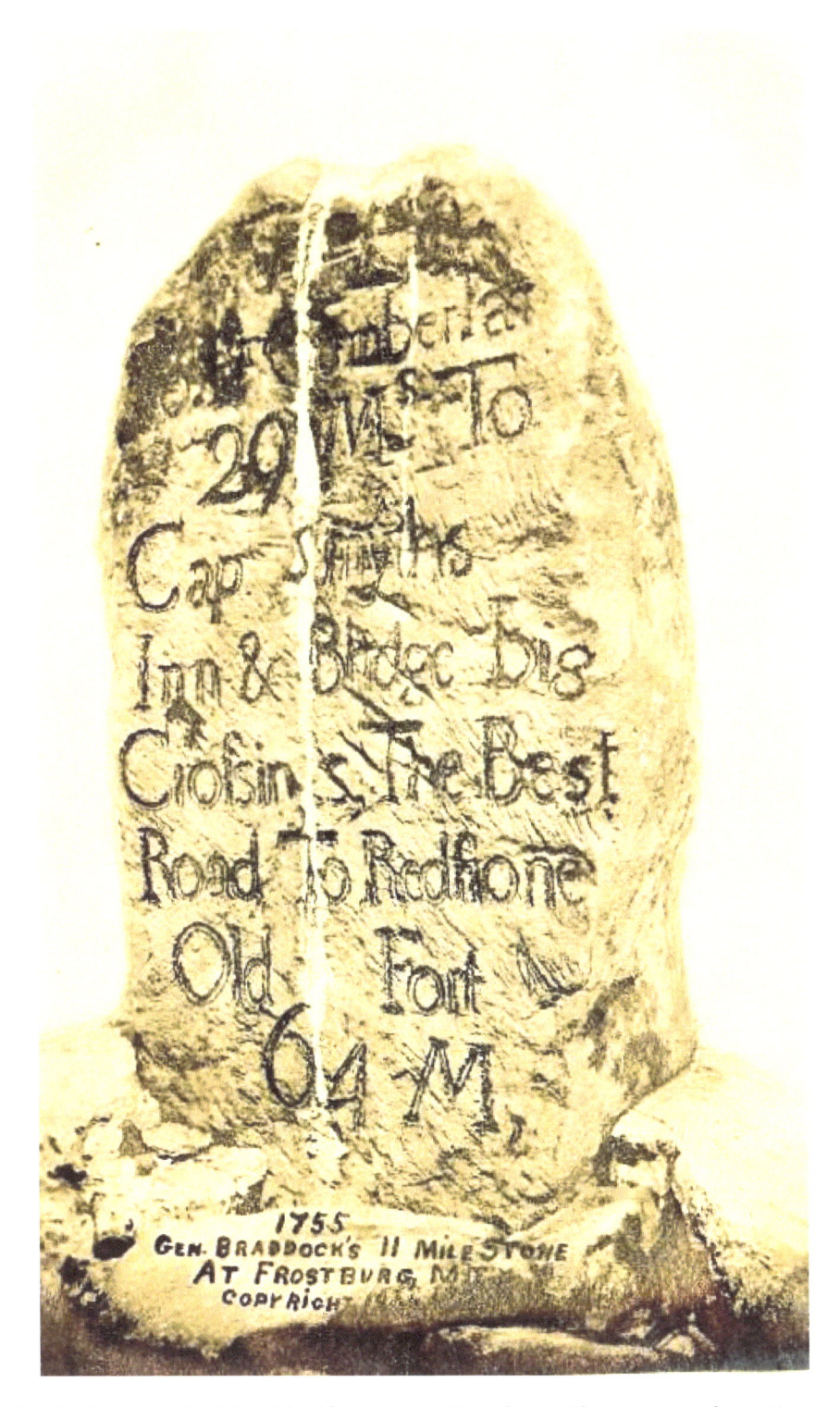

Figure 36 — This is the so-called Braddock's stone at Frostburg. The image is from the Lacock postcard series. The stone has nothing to do with General Braddock, and is simply a milestone. Uria Brown's 1816 journal, which is reproduced in Volume X of the 1915 "**Maryland Historical Magazine**", describes lodging at Phillip Smyth's Inn on the east side of the *"big Crossings"* of the Youghiogheny River. The stone could easily be interpreted as a roadside advertisement for Smyth's Inn and bridge.

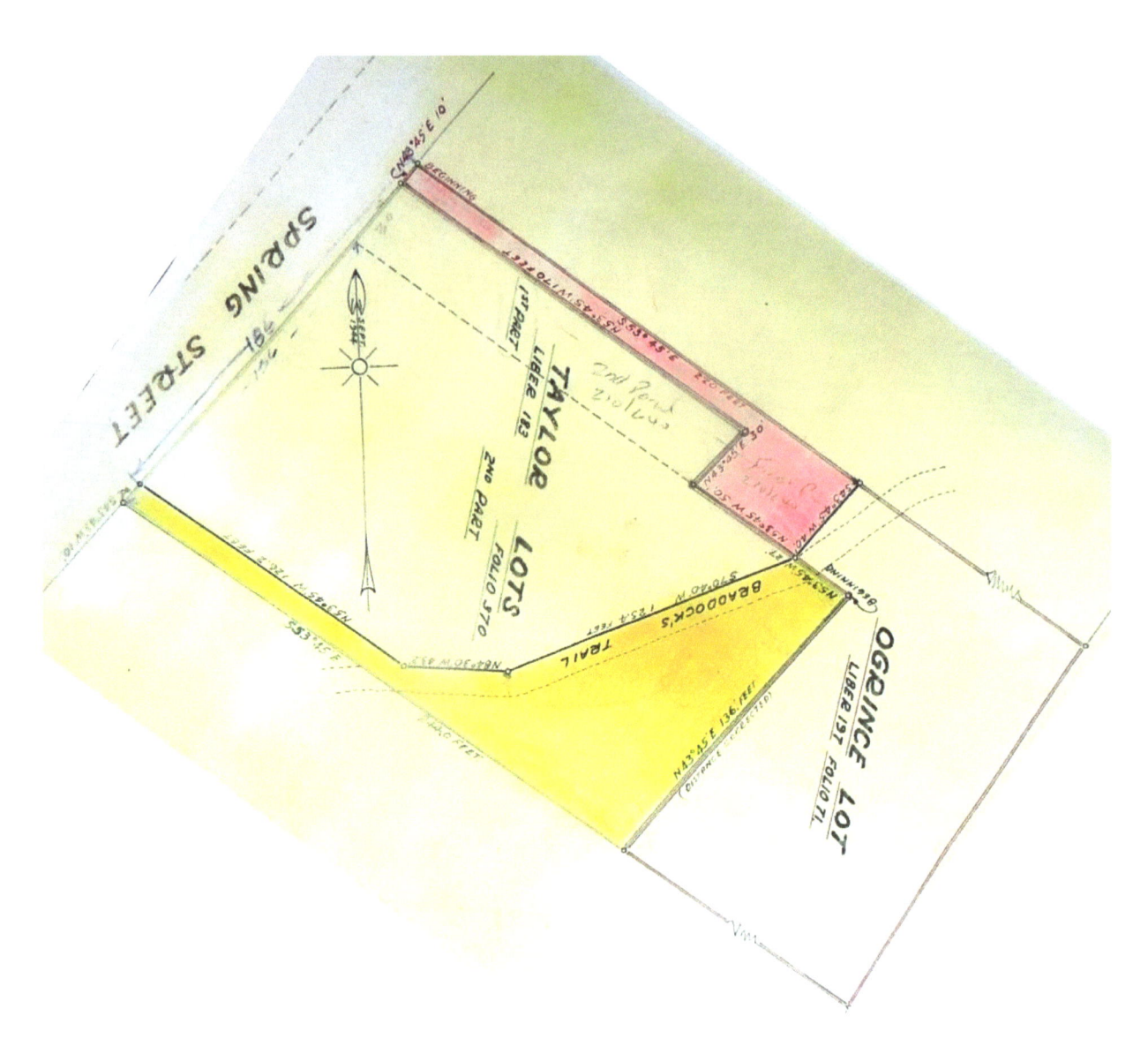

Figure 37 — This is a survey of a lot in Frostburg that illustrates the traditional route of Braddock's road. The portion where the words *"Braddock's Trail"* are located still survives as a sunken roadbed on a relatively steep hillside. The second camp was probably located on the high ground west of this hillside.

Figure 38 — This image of Braddock Park from the Braddock Road postcard series shows that the park is reasonable ground for a campsite. The text on the back of the postcard includes the statement, *"About 150 yards north of this park is an old mile stone."*

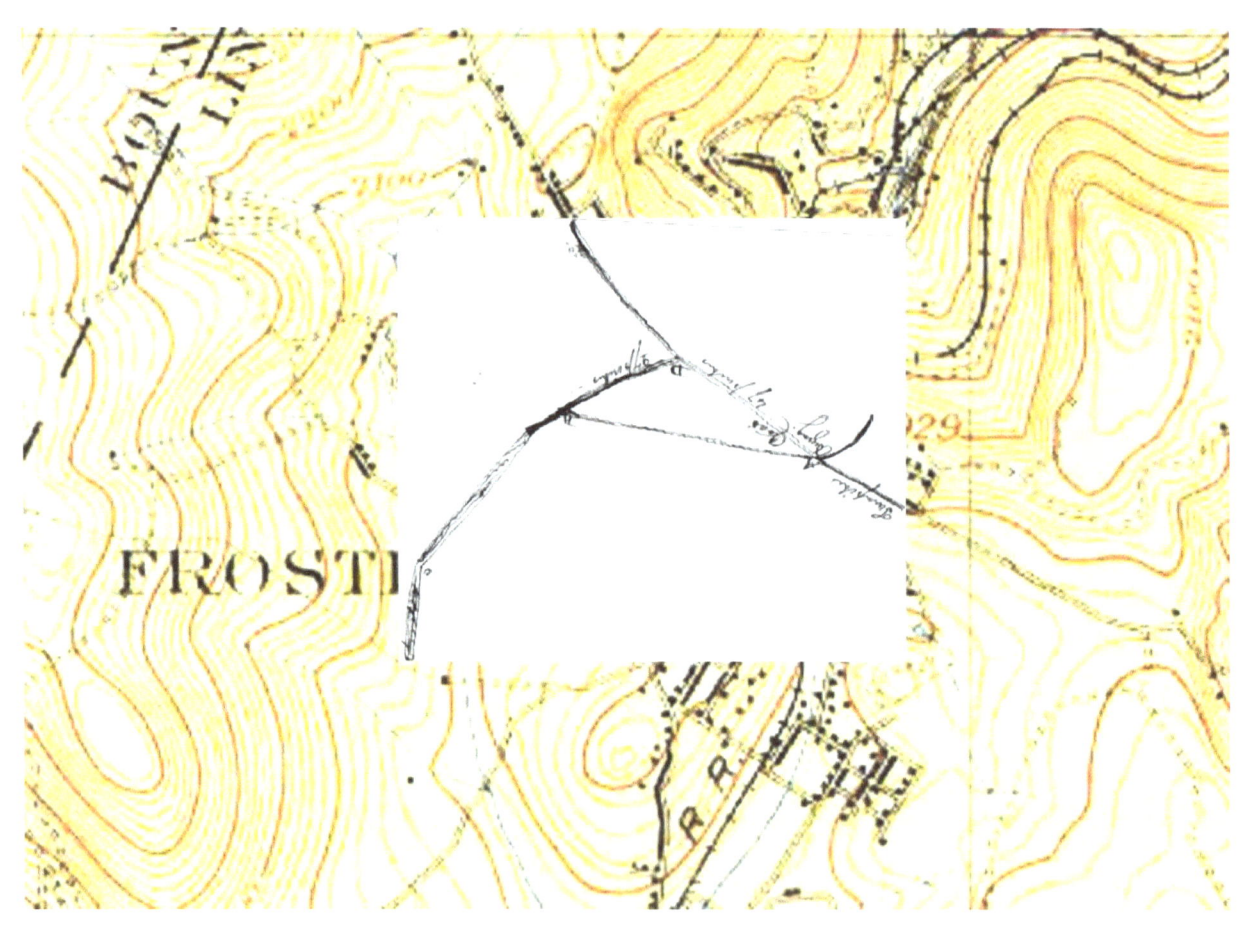

Figure 39 — The inset is from an August 19, 1819 survey that illustrates a road from the National Road to Christian Musselman's tavern on Braddock's road. The scale of the inset may be slightly off, mispositioning the southern end of the road by a few yards east or west at Musselmans, but seems to be substantially correct. This survey proves that the traditional route of Braddock's road through Frostburg was already known as Braddock's road in 1819. The survey states, *"Beginning at the Turnpike Road above Josiah Frosts, thence to run with said turnpike road by Meshach Frost's dwelling house forty-seven perches, then with a straight line of twenty seven perches to the old road leading to Christian Musselman's Tavern on Braddocks Road as will appear by a plat hereto annexed and we are of the opinion that the said road, when made publick will be of considerable benefit..."*[120]

---

[120] The survey transcript was provided by the late Steve Colby. The survey plat was provided by Judy Metz.

13. A perplexing 1756 letter from Thomas Cresap

Introduction

Previous material in this book proves that the Ohio Company cut a road westward from the mouth of Wills Creek that was followed, at least in general, by Braddock's 1755 expedition. This brief chapter quotes from a letter that suggests, but by no means proves, that there was only one road heading westward from the site of Clarysville in 1756, prior to the various improvements to Braddock's road that commenced in 1758. This in turn, suggests that Braddock's expedition followed the Ohio Company road west from the site of Clarysville.

Thomas Cresap departs from the road somewhere near Clarysville

An article titled *"Extract of a Letter from Colonel Cresap, dated June 6, 1756"* was published in the June 17, 1756 issue of the **"Pennsylvania Gazette"**, and includes the statement:[121]

> *On the 20th, I set off from Fort Cumberland with 71 volunteers... We marched the first Day about 8 miles, and encamped on a Branch of Will's Creek, when we killed a fat Bear.*
>
> *Next day we set off towards the Little Meadows through the woods, but finding that Way very bad, struck into the Road[122] at George's Creek, and marched on till we came to the Place on Savage River where my Son, Thomas Cresap, had the Engagement with the Indians...*

Analysis

This letter seems to suggest that Cresap's party camped at or near the site of Clarysville on the evening of May 20, 1756, and on the morning of May 21, 1756, followed whichever valley Braddock's road did not follow. Finding that way bad, they fell back into Braddock's road at Georges Creek. Whether this interpretation is correct is impossible to know, but it seems like a good possibility because men tend to follow terrain features that create avenues of least resistance. If the interpretation happens to be correct, it suggests that Braddock's road and its antecedent, the Ohio Company road, did not follow separate valleys westward from Clarysville.

The letter seems to indicate they were attempting to strike off for Little Meadows through the woods, rather than follow Braddock's road there. If Braddock's road followed Lacock's projected route, and Cresap followed Porter Run as a way to get to the Little Meadows without following Braddock's road, the letter doesn't make much sense, because going that way would simply return them to Braddock's road at Georges Creek. If Braddock's road followed Porter Run, and Cresap followed Preston Run hoping to get to Little Meadows without following Braddock's road, the letter makes more sense, because they could have logically planned to travel through the woods, paralleling Braddock's road.

---

[121] This was transcribed and forwarded to the author by Robert L. Bantz.
[122] The way this is stated, I take it to be a reference to the road they were following before they set off through the woods. In other words, I believe they were following Braddock Run, rather than Jennings Run, before setting off through the woods.

We can't put too much weight on this letter, because trying to make sense of it requires conjecture. I include it only because I recognize the degree that terrain influences the routes men take. Anyone following Braddock Run westward from Wills Creek at any period of human habitation has been faced with two choices: To follow Porter Run or Preston Run, in order to avoid the hill that is located just west of Clarysville.[123]

---

[123] This observation was made by Scott Williams.

14. The fly in the ointment: The 1760 Mountain survey

The Mountain tract[124] (Figure 40) was surveyed by John Murdock for Michael Cresap on September 10, 1760, and is outlined on Figure 12. The survey includes the statement, *"...I have carefully laid out for and in the name of the Said Cresap all that Tract of Land called The Mountain, lying in the af^d County, Beginning at two bounded white oaks standing on the point of a hill between the Main Branches of Georges Creek, about four hundred perches Northward of Braddocks road..."* Figure 12 shows the beginning point of the survey is located just west of Spring Street, on East College Avenue, approximately at latitude 39.650300°, longitude -78.925180°, and shows the traditional route of Braddock's road passing through the Mountain tract.

Four hundred perches is equal to 1.25 miles, yet the starting point of the Mountain tract is only about 363 yards north-northwest of the location where the traditional route of Braddock road crosses Spring Street. If the 400 perches statement is accurate, then Braddock's road would have instead been located approximately at latitude 39.632157°, longitude -78.925039°, on a hillside about 142 yards south of the present-day National Freeway (Route 68), about 710 yards (0.4 miles) west of the western end of Hoffman Hollow, and about the same distance west of the Route 36 interchange with Route 68. This is 2.06-miles west-southwest of Clarysville, and in no way fits with the route illustrated by the circa 1759/60 map, the *"Gordon map"*, at least one of the maps by Gist, the *"Orme map"*, and the Shippen map. It is also well to the west of the hard-right turn postulated by Lacock. The Mountain survey doesn't appear to vindicate Atkinson and Middleton either, in view of the 1793 session law that places Braddock's road directly on the Mountain tract. If it weren't for the aforementioned maps, one would have to wonder if the four hundred perches reference on the 1760 Mountain survey means that the traditional route of Braddock's road through the Frostburg area was a later route variation that took on the name of the older road. Those maps, which show the road crossing the head forks of Braddock Run, seem to rule out that possibility.

One can only guess that the road mentioned on the Mountain survey may relate to a different road that the surveyor, John Murdock, somehow confused with Braddock's road, or else he reported the wrong distance between the starting point and Braddock's road[125], or perhaps it was an early alteration to Braddock's road that was already known by the same name — or perhaps some unknown contingent of Braddock's forces did pass through Hoffman Hollow, but did not turn hard right (generally north) immediately after exiting Hoffman Hollow.[126] In particular, one might wonder if the phrase *"open a new road"* in Bouquet's previously referenced November 27, 1759 letter to Richard Paris has anything to do with the route of Braddock's road that is identified on the September 10, 1760 Mountain survey.

---

[124] The survey was provided by Judy Metz. This survey started the discussion that led to the creation of this book.
[125] This distance mistake theory was suggested by Judy Metz.
[126] This theory is based on comments provided by Scott Williams, who suggested that a second road, following the tributary of Preston Run through Hoffman Hollow, may have already existed at the time of the Mountain survey.

Conclusion

I believe the Mountain survey can be discounted, in view of the overall weight of evidence indicating the Ohio Company road, and Braddock's expedition, passed through the site of present-day Frostburg.

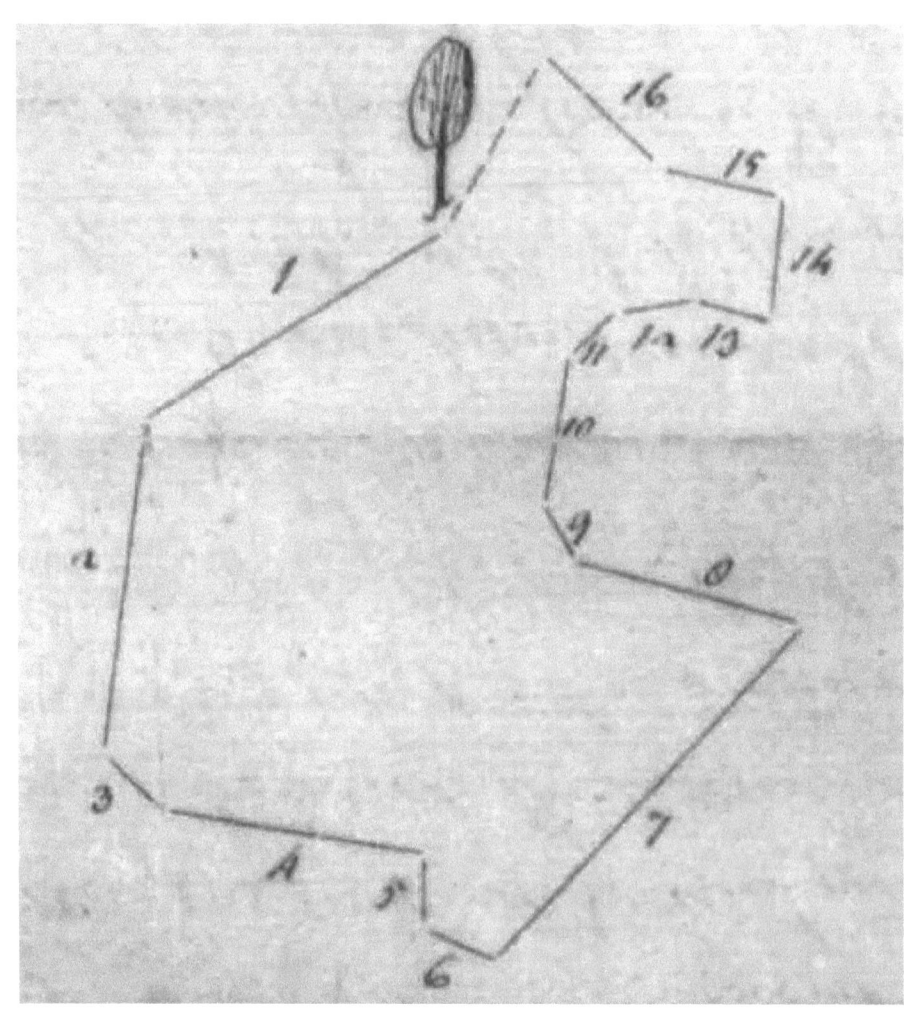

Figure 40 — This is the image from the September 10, 1760 Mountain survey. The starting point of the survey is identified with the icon of a tree.

15. Local tradition

The Seifarth tradition of Nemacolin's trail near the village of Eckhart Mines

Grace DePollo's book "**The History of the Seifarth Family of Eckhart Mines, Maryland**" includes an article titled *"I remember my Grandmother Seifarth"* that was written by Lola (Seifarth) Bachtel in 1985.[127] Lola was born in Eckhart in 1906, and was a graduate of the Normal School at Frostburg (now Frostburg State University). This probably means that she traveled regularly between Eckhart and Frostburg.

The beginning of the article gives an excellent description of where Lola's grandmother A. Elizabeth (Hagar) Seifarth's house was located in the 1920s.[128] Starting from Kelly's pump[129] on Route 40, the author describes taking Washington Hollow Road and passing under the railroad trestle, and then turning right up a steep path that led from the trestle to her grandmother's house. The trestle was located at latitude 39.649°, longitude -78.896°. The author stated that the house could be reached either by following the path from the trestle, or by following a railroad cut that is located at latitude 39.650°, longitude -78.897°. This seems to put the house somewhere near the western end of the railroad cut.

The house is described as being located on a relatively large piece of fairly flat ground that was situated at the base of what the author refers to as a *"high wooded area"*; see Figure 41. The description is sufficiently detailed to understand that the wooded area was somewhere on the northeastern end of the hill that forms the western flank of Washington Hollow, and most likely within the grounds of the present-day cemetery. The author then states that Nemacolin's trail was located in the wooded area, and connected with *"Braddock's rock"*, which the author associated with the Revolutionary War period.

The wooded area was located more than a mile from the starting point of the Walnutt Levill survey, so at the very least, the trail in the wooded area is harmonious with the reference to Nemacolin's road in the Walnutt Levill survey. The terrain in the vicinity of the railroad cut is steep, but if the path to the grandmother's house climbed up that steep hillside as described, perhaps Braddock's expedition did too, since Orme wrote that the road between the first and second camps was *"excessively mountainous"*.

One historian, who I very much respect, argued against the theory presented in this book by stating that he studied the ground between the village of Eckhart Mines and Grahamtown thoroughly, but did not find any evidence of an abandoned connecting road. The Seifarth article describes a trail that was known to local people in the 1920s, and one of them reported it as connecting the village of Eckhart Mines to *"Braddock's rock"*, which seems to be a reference to the Braddock Road milestone in Frostburg. What we cannot know with confidence is whether the connecting route statement is based on something the author had personal knowledge of or heard from her elders[130]

---

[127] The Seifarth article was provided by Scott Williams, who reports that his mother helped to prepare the book.
[128] Scott Williams reports that A. Elizabeth (Hagar) Seifarth died in 1930.
[129] Kelly's pump is a public spring that is located at latitude 39.649864°, longitude -78.895333°.
[130] I was born in 1953, and was told stories by my elders that dated back to the 1850s and 1880s, and passed through several generations before reaching my ears. One story was about a family that moved out west, discouraged that

in the 1920s, or something she added as an embellishment in 1985, based on exposure to one of the various pieces of literature that describe Braddock's expedition following Nemacolin's trail. This unanswerable question can also be turned inside out. It could very well be that the trail in the wooded area was known locally as Braddock's trail, and the author described it as Nemacolin's trail as an embellishment, based on exposure to literature that describes Braddock's expedition following Nemacolin's trail. We can't even be completely certain that the term *"Braddock's rock"* is a reference to the old Braddock Road milestone (Figure 36) in Frostburg, because there is a planted standing stone along Washington Hollow Road that some 50 years ago used to be referred to by locals as *"the real Braddock stone"*.[131]

It is sensible to acknowledge such potential issues, rather than wholeheartedly accepting tradition. No matter how much skepticism we apply, however, we are still left with one key fact. There was a trail in the wooded area, and whether it was known as Braddock's trail or Nemacolin's trail in the 1920s, its location is harmonious with the theory presented in this book.

The grandmother A. Elizabeth (Hagar) Seifarth is the likely source of the tradition, because her husband died circa 1898, before their granddaughter Lola was born. Elizabeth was born in Verna, Hesse in 1846, and emigrated to Frostburg in 1866. She married John Henry Seifarth in 1868, and they lived at the described house in Eckhart. Having lived in the area since the 1860s, she likely would have known people whose memory stretched back to the early 1800s. While the potential issues acknowledged above can't be disproven, it also may be possible that Elizabeth knew people with first-hand knowledge that the trail continued on to the milestone in Frostburg. It may even be possible that the author, Lola, walked part of the trail routinely as a significant shortcut to the National Road, while attending the Normal School at Frostburg.[132] Without a doubt, the traditional route of Braddock's road through Frostburg passed right by that school — and without a doubt, Lola wouldn't be the only person who ever routinely walked between the village of Eckhart Mines and Frostburg.

---

three children died in short order. Years later, a memorial to those children was found at a little cemetery in Tama County, Iowa. Another story was about an ancestor, Daniel Korns, who had to go to Philadelphia to get the money he was owed for the sale of his farm in Richie Hollow. Years later, I found a book of court cases showing that he won a property-related lawsuit known as *"Patrick's Appeal"* that was ruled on in 1884 by the Pennsylvania Supreme Court, in Philadelphia.

[131] Judy Metz provided the information about the standing stone that is located along Washington Hollow Road. It appears to have been cut by drilling a row of shallow holes (roughly 2.75" to 3.00" deep), and then using wedges to split the rock (Scott Williams provided information on the *"feather and wedge"* rock splitting technique). If I had to venture a guess as to what the stone was for, I would guess that it was a property boundary marker. I would also guess that people who lived in the area in the 1800s would have likely known the purpose of the stone, rather than connecting it with the Revolutionary War period.

[132] It may seem odd to suggest that someone might take such a shortcut, rather than follow the roads. My grandfather Irvin Henry Dietle, born in 1899, routinely walked across a number of fields and through some woods to teach at the one-room school at Wittenburg, Pennsylvania, as a significant shortcut to following the roads. By the roads, the distance is about 2.9 miles. By taking the shortcut, he saved a mile or so of walking each way. Rather than following the roads, he used a sleigh following the same general route when he moved his family and his possessions to the farm where he lived throughout his long teaching career. He lived in Larimer Township, Somerset County, Pennsylvania, on White Oak Hollow Road approximately at Latitude 39.783505°, Longitude -78.896553°. The Wittenburg one-room schoolhouse is located at Latitude 39.786803°, Longitude -78.928182°.

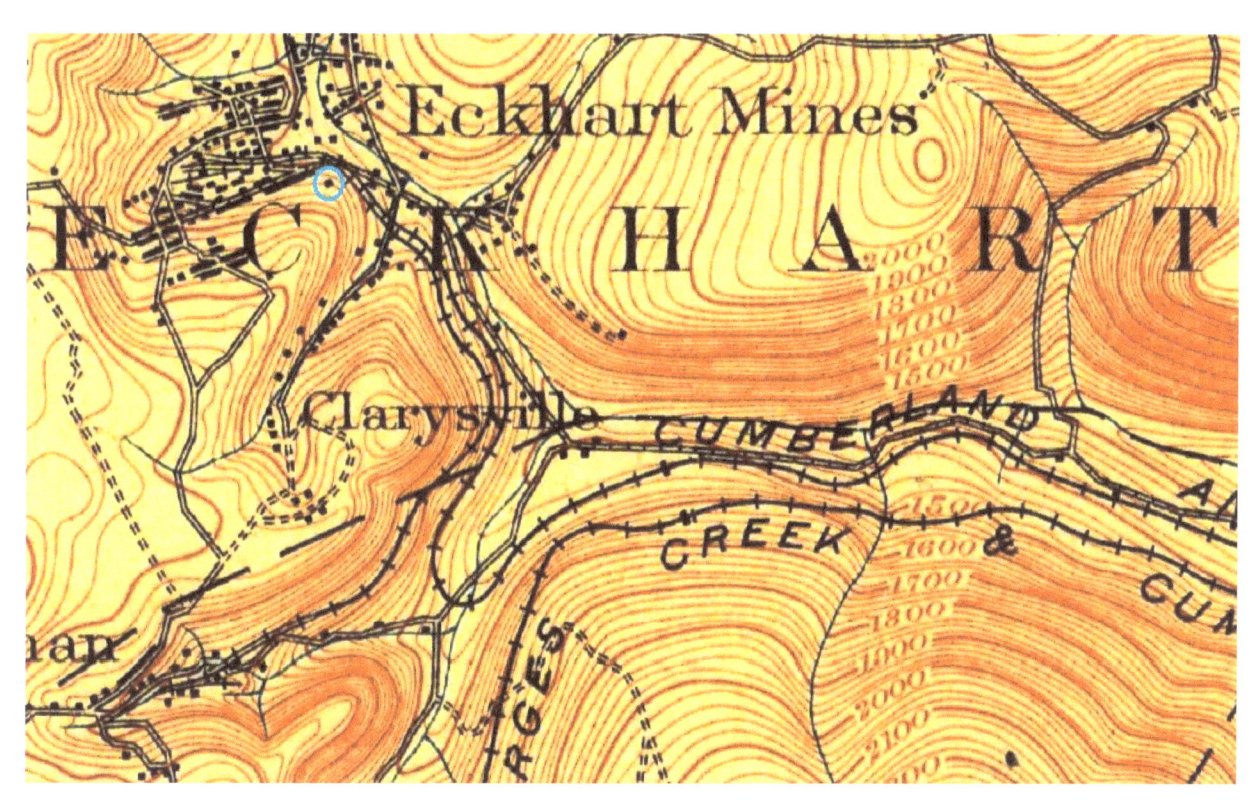

Figure 41 — This is from the 1908 topographical map of the area. The referenced home of A. Elizabeth Hagar Seifarth seems to the one circled in blue, because that house could have been reached by a path from the trestle that crossed Washington Hollow Road, or by following the railroad cut. Regardless of precisely where the house was located, the trail referenced by the Seifarth article was located somewhere on the northeastern end of the hill that is located at the letter "C" in the capitalized word "ECKHART".

16. Conclusion

Retrospective

I suspect that Lacock followed Middleton's map of Atkinson's study into Hoffman Hollow (he says so) as a result of a misinterpreting the second report of the commissioners for the National Road (which he quotes), and as a result of not having access to the then undiscovered maps of Christopher Gist — but then he had to deviate from the route illustrated on Middleton's map in order to incorporate the route shown on the Taylor survey (he mentions the Taylor property), and in order to incorporate the rest of the traditional route through the Frostburg area (see the other Frostburg-area property owners Lacock mentions). With Lacock's input, a very detailed map of his projected route between Clarysville and Frostburg was included in Bruce's book "**The National Road**", and the route shown on that map became the consensus route of Braddock's expedition that other historians accepted.

My personal conclusion

This book presents a theory suggesting that Braddock's expedition may have followed Porter Run, and camped between the head forks of Georges Creek. It is time now to seek additional evidence that may validate or repudiate this theory. As for me, I'm already convinced by the detail provided on the *"Gordon map"*, when viewed in the context of statements by Washington and Mercer indicating that Braddock followed the Ohio Company road, and considered in light of the Walnutt Levill survey, and considered in light of the route of the Ohio Company road through the site of Frostburg that is illustrated on Washington's map and the 1755 Fry and Jefferson map. To those who remain unconvinced by the information presented herein, I ask only that they provide at least a smidgeon of evidence that Braddock's expedition followed the primitive road Atkinson found in Hoffman Hollow. Until then, I submit that *some* evidence, even if it only consists of old out of scale maps, contemporaneous written documents, and a survey, seems to carry more weight than mere terrain-based conjecture.

17. Epilogue

Why is Braddock's road something that still interests so many people today? Hilaire Belloc summed up the allure of old roads to my satisfaction in 1924:

> *It is the Road which determines the sites of many cities and the growth and nourishment of all. It is the Road which controls the development of strategies and fixes the sites of battles. It is the Road which gives its framework to all economic development. It is the Road which is the channel of all trade and, what is more important, of all ideas. In its most humble function it is a necessary guide without which progress from place to place would be a ceaseless experiment. It is a sustenance without which organized society would be impossible; thus ... the Road moves and controls all history.*

The Ohio Company road, followed by Braddock in 1755, fits Belloc's statement as well as any road ever built in the course of human history, because it helped to set in motion a series of events that ultimately led to British control of a broad swath of North America. Although Braddock's expedition was an utter failure, the road he followed is one of two that opened the way for the settlement of southwestern Pennsylvania. Later, it served as the prototype for part of the National Road. Due to its influence on the trajectory of history, it is only fitting that we study its route.

Printed in the USA
CPSIA information can be obtained
at www.ICGtesting.com
CBHW041336010324
4848CB00033B/354